J. G. Swift MacNeill

The Irish Parliament

What It Was, And What It Did

J. G. Swift MacNeill

The Irish Parliament
What It Was, And What It Did

ISBN/EAN: 9783744734585

Printed in Europe, USA, Canada, Australia, Japan

Cover: Foto ©ninafisch / pixelio.de

More available books at **www.hansebooks.com**

THE

IRISH PARLIAMENT:

What it Was, and What it Did.

BY

J. G. SWIFT MACNEILL, M.A.,

CHRIST CHURCH, OXFORD; BARRISTER-AT-LAW, PROFESSOR OF CONSTITUTIONAL
AND CRIMINAL LAW IN THE HONOURABLE SOCIETY OF
THE KING'S INNS, DUBLIN

THIRD EDITION.

CASSELL & COMPANY, LIMITED:

LONDON, PARIS, NEW YORK & MELBOURNE.

1886.

PREFACE.

THERE are many versions of the British Parliament: it has had but one counterpart—that of Ireland. The Legislatures of the Colonies and Dependencies of Great Britain, where they are representative, have each, it is true, been modelled on the legislature of the mother country. They each, however, in outward form and structure, consciously depart from their original. Each colony has the Sovereign of Great Britain for its head, while the more important ones have a legislative Council or Senate analogous to the British House of Lords, and a Legislative Assembly analogous to the British House of Commons. In no instance, however, are any of the Colonial Legislative Councils framed on the hereditary principle. In some cases their members are nominees of the Crown, and hold office for life. In others, the Legislative Councillors hold office for a term of years, and are elected by electors having a property or educational qualification. In no instance is there a trace of a spiritual peerage. The Colonial Legislative Assemblies or Lower Houses are elected either by universal suffrage, or by electors having certain property or educational qualifications. In no instance is the franchise the same as the British Parliamentary franchise.

Ireland, on the other hand, had, like England, its hereditary House of Peers. In England and in Ireland, the laws regulating the Parliamentary franchise, were, before the Union, exactly the same. The similarity of the Irish and English Constitutions was thus described by Mr. Flood, in the Irish House of Commons :—"Ireland had," he said, "a Parliamentary constitution the same as that of England, with an hereditary and ennobled branch of the legislature, invested with final judicature, above three hundred years before any colony in America had a name. Those colonies have had popular assemblies, it is true, but not parliaments consisting of king, lords, and commons, with all the powers belonging to them." *

"From the earliest introduction," says Mr. Butt, "of the power of the English kings into Ireland, the Irish, who submitted to the rule of those kings, had a right to the same Parliamentary constitution as that which England enjoyed." "The Irish Parliament had, like the English Parliament, its hereditary House of Peers. Its House of Commons was elected exactly like the English House of Commons, by the freeholders of the counties, and by cities and towns deriving their right to return members from the charters of kings. The freehold franchise was the same in both, and the royal charters had exactly the same effect

---

* "Irish Debates," vol. i. p. 422.

and were construed and tried by the same rules of law." *

But while the machinery of legislation was the same, the development of the great principles which lie at the root of the British constitution was in the two countries widely different. Thus, for instance, the struggle between the prerogative of the Crown and the rights of the people culminated in England in 1688 in the expulsion of the Stuart dynasty. Ireland was, however, governed for nearly a century after that Revolution on the principles of the Stuarts. In England the constitutional struggle was between the monarch and the Parliament. In Ireland the contest lay between the Irish Parliament and the English Ministry. After the Revolution the English Ministry, who saw themselves dependent on the English Parliament, used the prerogatives wrested by that Parliament from the Stuarts, in the attempt to destroy the independence and enfeeble the powers of the Irish Legislature. The aim of the Irish patriot party in and out of Parliament was to extend to Ireland the rights gained by England at the Revolution, and thus to assimilate in spirit as well as in form the Irish to the English Constitution. "You struggled," said Grattan in the Irish House of Commons, "for the British Constitution in opposition to the claim of the British Parliament." † The aim of the English Government was, on the contrary, to make the

---

* " Proceedings of the Home Rule Conference, 1873," pp. 6, 7.
† " Irish Debates," vol. xv. p. 5.

Irish Constitution, in the words of Fox, speaking in the English House of Commons, "a mirror in which the abuses of the English Constitution are strongly reflected ;"* or, to use the words of Mr. Forbes, in the Irish House of Commons, "a system which tended to adopt all the defects of the British Constitution, and rejected all its excellences and advantages."† "I allow," said Grattan, "the British Constitution the best, and I arraign this model as the worst because practically and essentially the opposite of that British Constitution."‡

The great differences between the Irish and the British Constitutions did not escape the observation of Edmund Burke. Writing to Sir Hercules Langrishe, a distinguished member of the Irish House of Commons, he observes, "The Revolution operated differently in England and Ireland in many and essential particulars. Supposing the principles to have been altogether the same in both kingdoms, by the application of those principles to very different objects, the whole spirit of the system was changed, not to say reversed. In England it was the struggle of the *great body* of the people for the establishment of their liberties against the efforts of a very *small faction* who would have oppressed them. In Ireland it was the establishment of the power of

---

* "British House of Commons," March 23rd, 1797. "Irish Debates," vol. xvii. p. 218. Mr. Fox's speech is reported in full in that volume of the "Irish Debates."
† "Irish Debates," vol. vii. p. 210.
‡ "Irish Debates," vol. xii. p. 6.

a smaller number at the expense of the civil liberties and properties of the far greater part, and at the expense of the political liberties of the whole. It was, to say the truth, not a revolution but a conquest, which is not to say a great deal in its favour." *

Further on in the same letter the writer observes : " The true Revolution to you—that which most intrinsically and substantially resembled the English Revolution of 1688—was the Irish Revolution of 1782." † " If gentlemen will consult our history," said Mr. Forbes, in the Irish House of Commons, " they will find there was not any settlement of the Constitution of Ireland at that period (1688) ; the security of our religion and property were the benefits which the Protestants of this kingdom derived from the Revolution, essential and important advantages, which justly entitle the event to commemoration ; but the endeavours of a certain description of men in this House to obtain a participation in the benefits of the Constitution of England at the Revolution, and in those measures which grew out of that settlement, have been constantly and successfully resisted by the present British Minister." ‡

The various points of contrast between the Irish and the British Constitutions were, as these quotations have shown, very frequently alluded to by the public men of the day, in both the British and the

---

* " Edmund Burke on Irish Affairs," edited by M. Arnold, p. 239.
† " Edmund Burke on Irish Affairs," edited by M. Arnold, pp. 234, 244.
‡ "Irish Debates," vol. xii. p. 193.

Irish Legislatures; and a general view of the Irish Constitution will, it is believed, be of interest at the present time. It will be useful to the student, who will see in the defects of the Irish system the measure of the value of the British Constitution. The public man, too, having regard to these defects, will, it is hoped, avoid, in any future modification of the relations between Great Britain and Ireland, the dangers which proved fatal to a former Irish Constitution.

In the following pages I will endeavour to sketch in outline the constitution of the Irish House of Lords (chapter i.) and of the Irish House of Commons (chapter ii.); the relation of the Irish to the English Crown (chapter iii.); the relation of the Irish to the English Parliament (chapter iv.); the relation of the Irish Parliament to the English and Irish Privy Councils before 1782 (chapter v.); the relation of the Irish Parliament to the English Privy Council after 1782 (chapter vi.); the Irish Administration, noticing specially the "fugacious responsibility," which mainly contributed to the destruction of the Irish Constitution by a transaction, declared by Fox to be, "with all the circumstances attending it, the most disgraceful that ever happened to that country"* (chapter vii.); while I will conclude with a statement of the leading

---

* "Hansard's Parliamentary Debates," vol. 6, pp. 127, 128, Feb. 3, 1806. Mr. Fox made this observation on a motion that a public monument should be erected to the memory of Lord Cornwallis, who died in India. The motion was opposed by Mr. O'Hara, on the ground that the deceased nobleman had carried the Irish Union by corruption.

points of difference in the laws and practice of the English and of the Irish Constitutions (chapter viii.).

In this inquiry I will, as far as possible, quote the remarks of contemporary statesmen on the workings of a Constitution with which they were familiar. Such remarks are always interesting; addressed to popular audiences they are not likely to be misunderstood; spoken in the presence of persons well acquainted with the facts, and without fear of contradiction, they are presumably correct.

CONTENTS.

THE IRISH PARLIAMENT.

CHAPTER I.

THE CONSTITUTION OF THE IRISH HOUSE OF LORDS.

THE Irish House of Lords consisted at the time of the Union of 228 temporal and 22 spiritual peers. In the reign of Elizabeth the total number of Irish temporal peers was 32. In 1681, at the close of the last administration of the Duke of Ormond, their number had increased to 119, making with the bishops a total of 141 lords. In 1790 the number of Irish peers, with the bishops, amounted to 200.* During Lord Cornwallis's Viceroyalty, 29 Irish peers were created; of these only 7 were unconnected with the question of the Union.† Many of the Irish temporal peers were Englishmen and Scotsmen, who had no connection with Ireland either by property or family. Some had never taken their seats in the House of Lords, and, indeed, had never been in Ireland. When Mr. Yelverton introduced the heads of a Bill for the modification of Poynings' Law, the measure was opposed, on the ground that it would diminish the

* Mountmorres's "Irish Parliament," vol. ii. pp. 215—220.
† A list of these creations is given in "The Cornwallis Correspondence," vol. iii. p. 318.

power of the Privy Council and increase the power
of the House of Lords.   More confidence, it was
urged, should be placed in the Privy Council,
"who were all men firmly attached to the country,
than in the House of Lords, many of whom were
strangers, and had not a foot of estate in it;
and yet could by proxy defeat the best-intended
acts of the Commons."*   Mr. Grattan, too, bitterly
complained of the foreign element in the House of
Lords, and asked in the House of Commons whether
Roman Catholic Irishmen were to be excluded from
privileges to which strangers were admitted.   " Look
to your Peerage," he said, " how many English and
Scots are daily made your law-givers.   Have you
remonstrated against this periodical list, which the
breath of a British Minister qualifies to give law and
judgment in Ireland without any connection with this
country whatever ?"†

The foreign element in the House of Lords was,
with all its grievances, less objectionable than the
native accessions to the Irish peerage.   It was the
system of the Government " by the sale of peerages to
raise a purse to purchase the representation, or rather,
the misrepresentation, of the people of Ireland." ‡
" Will any man say," says Flood, "that the Constitution is perfect, when he knows that the honour of the

---

* See Mr. Gamble's speech, " Irish Debates," vol. i. p. 168.
† " Irish Debates," vol. xvii. p. 78.
‡ See Fox's speech in the British House of Commons, March 23,
1797, " Irish Debates," vol. xvii. p. 212.

peerage may be obtained by any ruffian who possesses borough interest?" * Grattan accuses the ministers of the Crown of having "introduced a trade or commerce, or rather brokerage of honours, and thus establishing in the money arising from that sale a fund for corrupting representation."† "The sale of peerages," says Curran, "is as notorious as the sale of cast-horses in the castle-yard ; the publicity the same, the terms not very different, the horses not warranted sound, the other animals warranted rotten."‡ "The Minister," says Mr. Grattan in another debate, "sells your Lords and he buys your Commons." § "The Irish Minister has taken money for seats in the peers under contract that it should be applied to purchase seats in the Commons."‖ "I have good reason to believe," says George Ponsonby, "that peerages have been sold for money, nay more, I have proof ; give me a Committee, and if I do not establish my charge degrade me, let me no more enjoy the character of an honest man. I dare you to it, and I risk my reputation on establishing the fact."¶ Edmund Burke, in a second letter to Sir Hercules Langrishe, speaks of the sale of peerages as a matter of notoriety. "I like Parliamentary reforms," he remarks, "as little as any man who has boroughs to sell for money or for peerages in Ireland."**
The sale of peerages and the purchase with the pro-

---

* "Irish Debates," vol. ii. p. 230. § "Irish Debates," vol. xi. p. 133.

† "Irish Debates," vol. x. p. 266. ‖ "Irish Debates," vol. xi. p. 135.

‡ "Irish Debates," vol. x. p. 290. ¶ "Irish Debates," vol. xi. p. 143.

** "Burke on Irish Affairs," p. 340.

ceeds of seats in the House of Commons, had become so usual, that when Lord Fitzwilliam, the most popular Lord-Lieutenant of Ireland, departed from the custom, and ennobled Lord Chief Baron Yelverton, Mr. Egan sarcastically inquired whether such conduct had led to his recall. "Was he recalled because he (Lord Fitzwilliam) disdained to sell peerages, to corrupt the House of Commons, as one of his predecessors had done,* and intended to send a character to the Upper House (the Chief Baron), than whom, travel east or west, none more deserving was to be found, as a contrast and corrective to the spawn and reptility that had crept into that august assembly."† "The peerage," Mr. Lecky feels himself constrained to say "which was the natural representative of the landed classes, was systematically degraded, and the majority of Irish titles are historically connected with memories not of honour, but of shame."‡

The alteration in the Constitution in 1782 gave, as will be subsequently explained, increased power to the Peerage. The advocates of popular rights understated the case when they said that peerages were sold, and members of the House of Commons purchased with the money obtained by the sale. The independence of the House of Lords was assailed by direct ministerial corruption. "The peers," writes the Duke of Rutland, then Lord Lieutenant of Ireland, in

* The Lord-Lieutenant here referred to is Lord Westmoreland.
† "Irish Debates," vol. xv. p. 148.
‡ "History of England in the 18th Century," vol. iv. p. 518.

a "most secret" despatch, dated 19th April, 1784, "under the new Constitution, have more power than before. Greater attention, therefore, and more expensive influence will be required, if we mean to direct its progress in the right way." "A share in the lucrative favours of Government must be set aside for the purpose of gaining attachments in that House, as the invention of mere external allurements will no longer maintain the influence which they may for the moment acquire. It will be absolutely incumbent on me to establish in the House of Lords the strongest and most immediate connection with a certain number of powerful members who may be at all times looked to, and may be depended upon, for the fidelity and firmness with which they will execute their trust."*

The spiritual peers were the Bishops of the Protestant Church. In Ireland, down to the middle of the eighteenth century, the Bishops, by reason of the number of absentee noblemen, commanded half the working majority in the House of Lords.† They were, however, entirely out of sympathy with the people. The hierarchy of Ireland, save in rare instances, were uniformly devoted to the Government, and "were supported by the lay peers, whom they moved as pawns on the chess-board."‡ They were zealous in the passing

---

* Froude's "English in Ireland," vol. ii. pp. 438, 439.
† Lecky's "England in the Eighteenth Century," vol. ii p. 225.
‡ Froude's "English in Ireland," vol. i. p. 381.

of the various penal statutes that disgrace the ferocious reign of Queen Anne, and the still more scandalous period of George I. On one measure only do we find the Bishops opposing Government, and then not as the friends, but as the enemies, of the people. The Government wished to mitigate, in the case of the Presbyterians, the horrors of the Penal Code. They accordingly strove to procure a repeal of the Test Act, which placed that loyal body under such grievous disabilities. Again and again Bills for the relief of Dissenters were strangled by the influence of the Bishops in the House of Lords. The Bishops were out of sympathy with the people for reasons easily perceived. They were aliens alike in religion, thought, feeling, and race. They were the nominees of the British Ministry; the Irish clergy had no voice in their selection. "During the eighteenth century every Primate of Ireland was an Englishman, as were also ten out of the eighteen Archbishops of Dublin and Cashel, and a large proportion of the other Bishops."* In 1769, out of the twenty-two Irish Bishops, fifteen were Englishmen.† In 1796 Mr. Grattan computed that half the Irish Episcopate were English. "Look," he said, "at your Bench of Bishops; one half, I believe, English." ‡ A visitor to the Universities of Oxford and Cambridge would be easily led, by the number of portraits of Anglo-Irish

* Lecky's "England in the Eighteenth Century," vol. ii. p. 228.
† Lecky's "England in the Eighteenth Century," vol. iv p. 375, note 2.
‡ "Irish Debates," vol. xvii. p. 78.

Bishops, "in artful folds of sacred lawn," which adorn the college halls, to conclude that the special mission of England during the eighteenth century was to evangelise ungrateful Ireland. Swift's description of the Irish Bishops of the middle of the eighteenth century must, it is feared, dispel this agreeable impression. He characterised them as highwaymen, who murdered on Hounslow Heath the gentlemen appointed to the Irish sees, stole their letters patent, came to Dublin, and were consecrated in their place.

At the close of the eighteenth century the episcopal character had not visibly improved. "The Church of Ireland," says Curran in 1787, "has been in the hands of strangers advanced to the mitre, not for their virtues or their knowledge, but quartered upon this country through their own servility or the caprice of their benefactors, inclined naturally to oppress us, to hate us, to defame us."* Commenting on the systematic exclusion of Irish Churchmen from the Bench, and more especially the disregard of the claims of Dean Kirwan, the most celebrated pulpit orator of the day, Grattan draws a full-length portrait of the Anglo-Irish Bishop of his period. "Had he (Dean Kirwan) been a blockhead, bred a slave, and trained up in a great English family, and handed over as a household circumstance to the Irish Viceroy, he would have been an Irish Bishop and an Irish Peer with a great patronage, perhaps

* "Irish Debates," vol. vii. p 193.

a borough, and have returned members to vote
against Ireland." *

* "Irish Debates," vol. xii. p. 17. These observations, it should
be remembered, are applied exclusively to the English ecclesiastics
billeted on the Irish Church. The persons who speak most
severely of the Anglo-Irish Bishops are loudest in their praises
of the faithful, suffering, and laborious Irish clergy. Curran, in
the next sentence after the one I have quoted, thus speaks: "The
real duties of religion have been performed by our own native
clergy, who, with all the feelings of gentlemen and scholars, have been
obliged to do the drudgery of their profession for forty, or at most, fifty
pounds a year, without the means of being liberal from their poverty,
without hope of advancing themselves by their learning or their virtues
in a country where preferment was notoriously not to be obtained by
either." Grattan's celebrated panegyric on Dean Kirwan is well
known. It occurs immediately before his description of the Anglo-
Irish prelates, " What is the case of Dr. Kirwan ? That man preferred
this country and our religion, and brought to both a genius superior
to what he found in either. He called forth the latent virtues of the
human heart, and taught men to discover in themselves a mine of
charity of which the proprietors had been unconscious. In feeding the
lamp of charity he had almost exhausted the lamp of life. He comes
to interrupt the repose of the pulpit, and shakes one world with the
thunder of the other. The preacher's desk becomes a throne of light :
around him a train not such as crouch and swagger at the levees of
princes (horse, foot, and dragoons), but that wherewith a great genius
peoples his own state—charity in action and will in humiliation,—
vanity, arrogance, and pride appalled by the rebuke of the preacher,
and cheated for a moment of their native improbity. What reward ?
St. Nicholas Within or St. Nicholas Without. The curse of Swift is
upon him—to have been born an Irishman—to have possessed a genius,
to have used his talents for the good of his country." Mr. Lecky observes that "the Catholics and Presbyterians in Ireland, though they
had many grievances, had at least one inestimable advantage. The
English Government had no control over the appointment of their
clergy." A remarkable article of recent date, attributed to the pen of
the Rev. Canon Travers Smith, ascribes to the English Government
the "attempted spiritual murder of the Irish Church." (See *Church
Quarterly Review*, January, 1885). The English interest was in truth
to the Irish Church what the rotten boroughs were to the Irish Parliament, a constant source of weakness, outrage, and disgrace.

Such being the constitution of the Irish House of Lords, some matters of procedure in which it differed from the English House of Peers are noteworthy. The members of both the English and Irish Upper Houses had the privilege of voting by proxy. In England, however, no peer who was not present was empowered to enter a protest on the Journals of the House. In Ireland peers could not only vote but protest by proxy.

In Strafford's Parliament, in 1634, the lords who had proxies were severally introduced, personating those whose proxies they had, and taking their seats according to their relative precedency. "This," says Lord Mountmorres, "is particularly mentioned because the right of protesting by proxy, which is a custom peculiar to the House of Lords of Ireland, seems to depend upon this circumstance, for as they personated those lords, so it seemed to follow that they should act in every respect for their proxies as if they were present, and, among other privileges, had a right to protest.*

A very interesting controversy arose a few years ago between the late Earl Cairns, when Lord Chancellor of England, and the Duke of St. Albans, as to whether the Lord Chancellor of England is *ex officio*

* "Mountmorres's "Irish Parliament," vol. i. pp. 321, 322. In 1865 Mr. Bagehot wrote, with respect to the House of Lords, "The abolition of proxies would have made the House of Lords a real house." "English Constitution," p. 125. In 1868 proxies were abolished by resolution.

Speaker of the House of Lords.* In Ireland the offices of Lord Chancellor and Speaker of the House of Lords, though in practice generally united, were regarded in theory as distinct. Thus, in the first session of Parliament after the Restoration the Primate, Archbishop Bramhall, and not the Lord Chancellor, was Speaker of the House of Lords.† The theoretical severance of the offices is brought prominently before us by the Duke of Rutland, as Viceroy, so late as 1784, wishing to create a Speakership of the House of Lords, with a salary attached, distinct from the Chancellorship.‡

Speaking of the English House of Lords, Lord Brougham says, that, according to the theory of the Constitution, " Every English peer on attaining twenty-one years, has as much voice on all the great questions which come before the House of Lords, as an ultimate court of appeal, as the Lord High Chancellor himself." Such is the theory of the Constitution, though in practice all is quite different. " The usage," he proceeds to observe, " is, and for a century has been, followed, with a single exception, for all but the law lords to abstain from taking any part, either on questions of appeal from Courts of Equity, or writs of error from Courts of Law, or in cases of peerage claims, which are regarded as questions of

* The correspondence and speeches are summarised by Professor Sheldon Amos : " Fifty Years of the English Constitution," pp. 101, 102.
† Mountmorres' " Irish Parliament," vol. i. p. 414.
‡ Froude's " English in Ireland," vol. ii. p. 440.

private right."* His Lordship then enumerates some
of the difficulties caused by the paucity of law lords
in the Upper House, and the contrivances which
their absence in his own time rendered necessary.†
In Ireland the theory of the Constitution and the
practice were the same. This was forcibly illustrated after the repeal of the English statute
of 6 Geo. I., which affected to deprive the
Irish House of Lords of their appellate jurisdiction, and to reduce them, in the words of
Mr. Grattan, "to a fashionable insignificance."‡
Viscount Strangford, Dean of Down, was, in 1784,
by a special statute, deprived from sitting in Parliament or making any proxy therein, and also
from sitting and voting on the trial of any peer. The
offence of this nobleman was that he acted criminally
and corruptly in writing, during the pendency of an
appeal in the House of Lords, to the father of one of
the litigants, asking for £200, "to enable him, by
daily appearance, to express his gratitude by doing
justice when he flattered himself to see success
crown the undertaking." §

* Brougham's " British Constitution," p. 359.
† Brougham's "British Constitution," pp. 359--363.
‡ "Irish Debates," vol. i. p. 335.
§ "23 and 24 Geo. III. c. 59. The letter is given in full in the
preamble of the statute.

CHAPTER II.

THE CONSTITUTION OF THE IRISH HOUSE OF COMMONS.

THE House of Commons for nearly a century previous to the Union consisted of three hundred members. Addressing that assembly on the question of Reform in 1793, Mr. Grattan thus described in its very presence its history and constitution.

" I will advert to the state of your representation ; it is short. Of three hundred members above two hundred are returned by individuals, from forty to fifty are returned by ten persons; several of your boroughs have no resident elector at all ; some of them have but one; and, on the whole, two-thirds of the representatives in the House of Commons are returned by less than one hundred persons." " In 1613 the members returned to Parliament were two hundred and thirty-two, since which time sixty-eight members have been added, all by the House of Stuart, one by Anne, four by James II., most of the remainder by Charles I. with a view to religious distinctions, and by Charles II. with a view to personal favour." " The form of your Constitution was twelve counties, established in the reign of King John. Henry VIII. added one, Mary two, and Elizabeth seventeen, since which time your counties received no addition whatever, though between the year 1613 and the present the borough interest has received an addition of sixty-eight members, which is more than double the whole county representation.

"The great division on this subject is cities or boroughs, where the grant was to burgesses and freemen indefinite, or to a limited number of burgesses, seldom exceeding twelve, in whom the right of election was confined. The former are boroughs intended to be free; the latter intended to be otherwise. The number of the former I apprehend to be above forty, and when they have become what we understand to be intended by the word 'close boroughs' they have departed from the intention of the grant, and ought, pursuant to the meaning of that grant, to be opened. The other class, which I apprehend to be above forty, are in their origin vicious, and it is a monopoly like any of the other monopolies of James I.—a grant in its nature criminal.* Most of the forty boroughs created by James I. were so. It appears from the grants themselves that they were intended to be private property. They were granted as a personal reward for doing some specified transaction." "Thus, there are these two descriptions of boroughs: the one intended

---

* Referring to the enfranchisement of close boroughs, Mr. Grattan in 1797 thus expressed himself in the House of Commons: "Thus by far the greater number of your boroughs, and near one half your representation, is not your ancient Constitution, but a gross and flagrant encroachment, and a violent usurpation of the worst family that ever trampled on the independency and fabric of representation."—"Irish Debates," vol. xvii. p. 563.

to be free by the grant and rendered close by the proprietor, the other intended to be close by the grant and rendered vicious by the principles of the law.

"As to the public welfare, I acknowledge many beneficial acts, wholesome regulations, and one great revolution ; but may I be suffered to think that the redemption of this country had been more speedily established, the good of this country more uniformly pursued, and with less intervals of incon-sistency, if Parliament had been constituted more according to the principle of the Constitution ? As it is constituted, to me its ordinary operation appears defective, its raptures successful, and its relapses dis-graceful."

"I have heard," said Mr. Grattan in the same debate, "that seats in this House forty years ago were obtained for £600. I have heard they now cost £3,000."*

On the same occasion Hely Hutchinson, the Provost of Trinity College, entered into an analysis of the representation of the people in the House of Commons. He contrasted the exercise of the preroga-tive in the enfranchisement of boroughs in Ireland with its practical abeyance in England since 1676. He said that in former times he had extracted from all the borough charters their material contents, and stated, as the result of his researches, that "one half of the representation of Ireland had arisen from the

* " Irish Debates," vol. xiii. pp. 160—163.

exertions of the prerogative, influenced by occasional motives, disputes amongst religionists, and inducements of personal favour." *

"The mandate of a borough monger," said Curran, " can return any man, however contemptible, however obnoxious, into this House." †

" Are there not many among us," said Mr. Thomas Sheridan, "who could not find the way to the place they represent, who never saw a constituent, who were never in a borough, who at times cannot recollect the name of it? He said he did not much relish or deal in anecdotes on serious subjects, but there was one which was true and very apposite. By a courtesy of the House of Commons in England members of the Irish Parliament are admitted to hear the debates. A friend of his, then a member, wishing to avail himself of the privilege, desired admittance. The door-keeper desired to know what place he represented. 'What place? Why, I am an Irish member.' 'Oh, dear, sir, we are obliged to be extremely cautious, for a few days ago Barrington, the pickpocket, passed as an Irish member.' 'Why, then, upon my soul, I forget the borough I represent; but if you get me Watson's Almanack I will show it to you.'" ‡

* "Irish Debates," vol. xiii. pp. 167, 168. In this speech Mr. Hutchinson related the well-known story that when a remonstrance was made to James I. on the impropriety of creating 40 Irish boroughs at a stroke, he replied, "I have made 40 boroughs; suppose I had made 400—the more the merrier !"

† "Irish Debates," vol. vii. p. 27.

‡ "Irish Debates," vol. xiii. p. 59.

"What shall we say," says Sir Laurence Parsons, "that we have been doing when we go back to our representatives? I ask pardon—I forgot. A majority of this House never go back to their representatives. They do not know them; they do not live among them; many of them never saw them—no, nor even the places that they represent. What a mockery is this of representation!" *

These statements, made in the House of Commons, were not exaggerated. At the time of the Union compensation was given to the patrons of eighty-four boroughs which were disfranchised, and which were considered in the light of private property, the owners receiving £7,500 for each seat.†

The differences between the English and the Irish House of Commons will be incidentally considered in the account which I propose to give of the laws of the Irish Constitution. The charge of corruption has been frequently brought against the Irish House of Commons. This charge could, with perhaps equal propriety, be levelled at the English House of Commons of the same period. The members of the Irish Legislature were, however, exposed to far greater temptations. "In England," said Mr. Flood, who was a member of both the English and the Irish House of Commons, "the Legislature has only to contend with the native power of Government, but

---

* "Irish Debates," vol. xiv. p. 103.

† See list of boroughs and sums paid to owners. "Cornwallis Correspondence," vol. iii. pp. 321—324.

we have here to contend against the mass of another great executive power." * It must be remembered too, as will be afterwards shown, that placemen and pensioners were not excluded from the Irish Parliament. No Place Bill was passed till 1793, and by its provisions members holding offices created since the date of its enactment were alone excluded. Nor was there till that year any appropriation of supplies. Pension and Place Bills, though frequently proposed, were strenuously resisted by the Government of the day for the purpose of corruption. "The number of placemen and pensioners sitting in this House," said Grattan in 1790, "equal near one-half of the whole efficient body." † "I rise," said Curran, in the same debate, "in an assembly of three hundred persons, one hundred of whom have places and pensions."‡

From the very constitution of the Irish Parliament corruption was inevitable. "The Irish Parliament," says Mr. Lecky, "was in truth a body governed very constantly by corrupt motives, though probably not more so than the English Parliament in the time of Walpole." § One of the most eloquent members of the Irish House of Commons traced, in the following words, the source of the corruption over which he mourned : "The gentlemen of this country," said Sir Laurence Parsons, from his place in Parliament in 1794, "if not poisoned by example and temptation,

---

* "Irish Debates," vol. v. p. 151.
† "Irish Debates," vol. x. p. 60.
‡ "Irish Debates," vol. x. p. 109.
§ "Rise and Influence of Rationalism in Europe," vol. ii. p. 123.

would be as virtuous as any on earth. It is their nature to be so. They are not born an avaricious, griping, plundering gentry; but the very reverse— noble, generous, and independent. It is only the most vile Government that makes any of them otherwise. It is the despicable panders of an external administration; who come over here and blow upon their characters, and tamper with them and taint them; and then, when they go back to England, stigmatise them for the very taint which they themselves had given, until they have made the name of the Irish Parliament almost a synonym for corruption."*

* "Irish Debates," vol. xiv. pp. 101, 102. For some account of Parliamentary corruption in England, see May's "Constitutional History," vol. i. pp. 361—387; Hallam's "Constitutional History," vol. iii. pp. 263—267.

CHAPTER III.

THE RELATION OF THE CROWN OF IRELAND TO THE CROWN OF ENGLAND.

HAVING described the constitution of the Irish Houses of Parliament, the Crown of Ireland next demands our notice.

The various relations between England and Ireland have been, with one exception, matters of controversy. The nature of the connection of the English and Irish Crowns has never been disputed. "It has ever been acknowledged," says Molyneux, "that the kingdom of Ireland is inseparably annexed to the Imperial Crown of England."* By the provisions of a statute passed in the 33rd year of Henry VIII.'s reign, the king of England is *ipso facto* king of Ireland.† The various statutes altering the succession of the Crown in England at and after the Revolution were not re-enacted in Ireland. When the English Parliament disposed of the English Crown they disposed likewise of the Irish Crown. The Irish Parliament, by the Act of Recognition, practically acknowledged England's right in this respect.‡

---

* "Case of Ireland," p. 86.

† By this statute Ireland is converted from a "lordship" into a "kingdom." The kings of England, who were previously "lords" of Ireland, are henceforth "kings" of the kingdom of Ireland, "as united and knit to the Crown of England."—33 Hen. VIII., Ir. c. 1.

‡ 4 Wm. and Mary, Ir. c. 1.

That "the Crown of Ireland is an Imperial Crown inseparably annexed to the Crown of Great Britain" forms one of the propositions in Mr. Grattan's celebrated address to the Crown of the 16th April, 1782.*

"The Crowns of both nations," says Mr. Flood, "are united by a strong bond, for by a law of our own it is declared that whoever wears the Imperial Crown of England shall also wear the Imperial Crown of Ireland."† "The Crown of Ireland and the Crown of England are inseparably and indissolubly connected," says Fitzgibbon.‡ "The principle of law is," says Mr. O'Connell in 1843, "that whoever is king *de facto* in England is king *de jure* in Ireland."§ Mr. Butt says that "O'Connell's language, though strong, was scarcely exaggerated," and that "this much at least is unquestionable, that, if by any legitimate authority, a right was acquired to the Crown of England, the person who became king of England was *de jure* sovereign of Ireland."‖

Now although, as Mr. Grattan observed, "the Irish Crown is annexed to, but not merged in, the Crown of England,"¶ this annexation entailed certain serious consequences which were keenly felt by Irish statesmen before the Union.

"The king is," in the words of Mr. Warren, "the

* "Irish Debates," vol. i. p. 337.
† "Irish Debates," vol. i. p. 452.
‡ "Irish Debates," vol. ix. p. 48.
§ "Report of Discussion in Dublin Corporation on Repeal of Union," p. 67.
‖ "Proceedings of Home Rule Conference," 1873, p. 8.
¶ "Irish Debates," vol. xi. p. 391.

visible representative of the majesty of the State."
"The king," says Edmund Burke, "represents the
whole contracting capacity of the nation; he acts as
the national procurator."* He is the representative
of the community as to sovereign States; has the sole
prerogative of making peace and war, of concluding
treaties, of acquiring dominions and colonies, of com-
manding the army and navy. The king of England,
however, exercised these great prerogatives as the
wearer not of the Irish but of the English Crown, and
under the advice not of an Irish but of an English
Cabinet. Ireland was, in the words of Wolfe Tone,
describing her condition in 1791, "without pride, or
power, or name; without ambassadors, army, or navy."
"In giving Great Britain the nomination of her
monarch," says Mr. Flood, "Ireland gives her in
effect the power of treating for her with all the world,
and of declaring peace and war for her with all
mankind. What follows: that Ireland can have no
enemies but those who are made so by Britain."†

"What name have we," says Sir Laurence Parsons,
"among the nations of the earth? Who fears us?
Who respects us? What notice have foreign States
of us? Where are our negotiators? Where are our
ambassadors? What treaties do we enter into?
What alliances do we form? With what nations do
we make peace or declare war? Are we not a mere
cypher in all these?" "We are an independent

* "Burke on Irish Affairs," p. 57.
† "Irish Debates," vol. v. p. 399

C

kingdom, true. We have an Imperial Crown distinct from England, true. But it is a metaphysical distinction—a mere sport for speculative men; nothing in act or efficiency. Who governs us? English ministers, or rather the deputies of English ministers—mere subalterns in office, who never dare to.aspire to the dignity of any great sentiment of their own." *

* "Irish Debates," vol. x. p. 244.

CHAPTER IV.

THE RELATION OF THE IRISH TO THE ENGLISH PARLIAMENT.

THE claim of the English Parliament to legislate for Ireland was hotly contested, and formed the basis of the great constitutional struggle which terminated in 1782. As this claim was absolutely renounced by England in 1783 it will not be necessary to enter minutely into the question. The English contention was that the dependence of the Irish Parliament on the English Parliament followed as a corollary from the dependence of the Irish on the English Crown. The 6 Geo. I., cap. 5 (English) enacts "That the kingdom of Ireland has been, is, and of right ought to be subordinate unto and dependent upon the imperial crown of Great Britain as being inseparably united and annexed thereunto, and that the King's Majesty, by and with the advice and consent of the Lords Spiritual and Temporal and Commons of Great Britain in Parliament assembled, had, hath, and of right ought to have full power and authority to make laws and statutes of sufficient force and validity to bind the people and kingdom of Ireland. It was further enacted that the House of Lords of Ireland have not, nor of right ought to have, any jurisdiction to judge of, affirm, or remove any judgment, sentence, or decree given or made in any Court within the said kingdom, and that all proceedings before the said House of Lords upon any such judgment, sentence, or decree are utterly null and void." Blackstone, too, in his Commentaries, lays it down as incontrovertible that Acts of the English Parliament extended into Ireland if it were specially named or included under such general words as "within any of the king's dominions." *

The Irish Parliament, while admitting the dependence of the Irish on the English Crown, repelled without qualification the theory of the subordination of the Irish to the English legislature. The address to the Crown moved in the House of Commons by Grattan on the 16th April, 1782, may be regarded as an authoritative declaration of Ireland's constitutional position, "To assure his Majesty that his subjects of Ireland are a free people, that the Crown of Ireland is an imperial Crown inseparably annexed to the Crown of Great Britain, on which connection the interests and happiness of both nations essentially depend ; but that the kingdom of Ireland is a distinct kingdom with a Parliament of her own, the sole legislature thereof ; that there is no body of men competent to make laws to bind this nation except the King, Lords and Commons of Ireland, nor any other Parliament which

* "Commentaries," Introduction, sect. 4. Blackstone was offered, but declined the post of Chief Justice of the Common Pleas in Ireland. Foss, "English Judges," p. 98.

hath any authority or power of any sort whatever in this country save only the Parliament of Ireland;" "To assure his Majesty that we have seen with concern certain claims advanced by the Parliament of Great Britain in an Act entitled an Act for the better securing the dependency of Ireland; an Act containing matter entirely irreconcilable to the fundamental rights of this nation. That we consider this Act and the claims it advances to be the great and principal cause of the discontents and jealousies in this Kingdom."[*]

Lord Chief Justice Whiteside, commenting on the Act of 6 Geo. I., coincides with the opinions advanced in Grattan's address. "This statute was," he writes, "a complete assertion of authority over the legislature and kingdom of Ireland, and a practical denial of its Parliamentary independence."[†] "It furnishes a decisive proof that whether the Tudor or the Stuart or the Guelph reigned, it was equally the policy of England not to permit the existence of an independent Parliament in Ireland."[‡]

The Act of the 6th George I. was repealed in 1782 by the British Parliament.[§] The mere repeal of this statute did not satisfy Mr. Flood, who contended that there should be a complete and absolute renunciation by the English Parliament of all claims to legislate for Ireland.

[*] "Irish Debates," i. p. 337.
[†] "Life and Death of Irish Parliament," p. 110.
[‡] "Life and Death of Irish Parliament," p. 114.
[§] 22 Geo. III. c. 53.

"It is an undeniable principle of law," he said, "that the mere repeal of a declaratory Act does not renounce the principle of it, and it is clear to common sense that nothing but a final renouncing of the principle of this law is adequate to our security. With regard to this law of George I. the maxim I have mentioned obtains with peculiar force. What is the title of the law? It is an Act for the better securing the dependency of Ireland. On the face of it, therefore, it imports expressly that dependency did before exist, and that by consequence it must continue after unless renounced. It had, indeed, too strong an antecedent existence to be destroyed by any weak implications. The first authority of law known to the English Constitution is that of the great Lord Coke; his authority is expressly against us and in favour of the English Parliament. Will any lawyer say that the clear and decided opinion of Lord Coke, in a matter of law, is to be contemned? Add to this a number of statutes made by the English Parliament and acquiesced in by the Irish nation, antecedent to the declaratory law of George I., and will any man be so rash, so foolish, or so corrupt, as to say that such pretension is to be overlooked? or that it can be rationally stated to be so void of principle and colour as that a bare repeal of a subsequent and declaratory Act can annihilate it?"*

Grattan, on the other hand, contended that the simple repeal of this statute was abundantly sufficient

* "Irish Debates," vol. i. pp. 417, 418.

to secure the complete legislative independence of Ireland, and the House inclined to this view. Lord Mansfield, in Michaelmas term, 1782, and after this discussion pronounced judgment in an Irish appeal. The case, however, had been carried to England long before the repeal of the Act 6 George I. Increased force was thus given to Mr. Flood's contention, which Lord Chief Justice Whiteside has pronounced to be well founded.* Complaints were made of Lord Mansfield's decision in the British House of Commons. On the 22nd January, 1783, Mr. Secretary Townshend moved accordingly for leave to bring in a bill, which subsequently became law, "for removing and preventing all doubts which have arisen or may arise concerning the exclusive rights of the Parliament and Courts of Ireland in matters of legislation and judicature, and for preventing any writ of error or appeal from any of his Majesty's Courts in that kingdom from being received, heard, or adjudged in any of his Majesty's Courts of the kingdom of Great Britain.† "Between 1782 and 1800 Ireland was," in the words of Sir G. C. Lewis, "legally an independent state, the king of which was also King of Great Britain, and its political relation to Great Britain was precisely similar to that which subsisted between England and Scotland in the interval between the union of the two crowns and the union of the two kingdoms."‡

* *See* "Life and Death of Irish Parliament," p. 129.
† 23 George III., c. 28.
‡ "Essay on Government of Dependencies," pp. 154, 155.

The real and great usurpations of the English
Parliament were not so much its interference with the
internal affairs of Ireland, but the Acts which were
framed for the purpose of destroying Irish manu-
factures, especially the woollen. The effect of this
legislation was to crush out all industrial enterprise.
By excluding the mass of the people from all
other means of livelihood except agriculture, it has
produced the land-hunger which is the fruitful source
of Ireland's disturbance and distress. Edmund
Burke, in a letter written in 1778 to gentlemen in
Bristol, denounced, in terms which lost him his seat
in Parliament for that city, England's destruction of
Irish industries. " Is Ireland," he asked, " united to
the Crown of Great Britain for no other purpose than
that we should counteract the bounty of Providence
in her favour, and, in proportion as that bounty has
been liberal, that we are to regard it as an evil which
is to be met with in every sort of corrective?"*

* " Burke on Irish Affairs," p. 101.

CHAPTER V.

THE RELATION OF THE IRISH PARLIAMENT TO THE ENGLISH AND IRISH PRIVY COUNCILS BEFORE 1782.

THE English Parliament did not directly, to any great extent, interfere in the internal affairs of Ireland. The Irish Parliament was, however, previously to 1782, efficiently controlled by the English Privy Council, who were themselves responsible to the English Parliament. In 1495, by an Act of the Irish Parliament known by the name of Poynings' Law, from the Lord Deputy in whose administration it was passed, amongst other provisions all the laws of England, antecedent to that date, are deemed good and effectual in Ireland.* This provision, which forms what Mr. Hallam calls an epoch in Irish jurisprudence, fades into insignificance in the light of the measure which gives its peculiar importance to Poynings' Law. It was further enacted that no Parliament shall in future be holden in Ireland till the king's lieutenant shall certify to the king, under the great seal, the causes and considerations and all such acts as it seems to them ought to be passed thereon, and such be affirmed by the king and his council, and his licence to hold a Parliament be

* 10 Hen. VII., Ir., c. 4.

obtained; and any Parliament holden contrary to
this form and provision should be deemed void.

In the 3rd and 4th Philip and Mary, an Act
was passed for the explanation of Poynings' Law, by
which permission was given to the Lord-Lieutenant
and Council, while the Parliament was sitting, to
certify to the King such provisions as they might
deem expedient to be framed into laws during a
session of Parliament.* A negative alone on the
provisions thus framed by the Council was left to
Parliament. After the explanatory Act of Philip and
Mary, a general proposition for a bill, by way of
address to the Lord-Lieutenant and Council, was
allowed to come from Parliament. But it was not till
after the Revolution of 1688 that the heads of bills
were presented; these resembled Acts of Parliament
or bills, with only the small difference of " We pray
that it may be enacted," instead of " Be it enacted."†
Conferences between the two Houses were very
usual, while Poynings' Law prevailed. As heads
of bills were recommended only by one House
it was desirable to induce the two Houses to
confer and to give efficacy to these propositions by
a joint recommendation.‡ When the heads of a bill
were peculiarly popular they were presented by Parliament in a body to the Lord-Lieutenant, with a
request that he would recommend the measure to ·

---

* 3 & 4 Ph. & Mary, Ir., c. 4.
† Mountmorres's " Irish Parliament," vol. ii. p. 142.
‡ Mountmorres's " Irish Parliament," vol. ii. 183.

the King. In practice the origination of bills in the Privy Council was confined to the case of the summoning of a new Parliament.* Lord Mountmorres thus distinctly states the procedure before 1782.

"Propositions for laws, or heads of bills as they are called, originated indifferently in either House. After two readings and a committal they were sent by the Council (that is the Irish Privy Council) to England, and were submitted usually by the English Privy Council to the Attorney- and Solicitor-General, and from thence they were returned to the Council of Ireland, from whence they were sent to the Commons, if they originated there (if not to the Lords), and after three readings they were sent up to the House of Lords, where they went through the same stages, and then the Lord Lieutenant gave the royal assent in the same form which is observed in Great Britain. In all these stages in England and Ireland it is to be remembered that any bill was liable to be rejected, amended, or altered, but that when they had passed the great seal of England no alteration could be made by the Irish Parliament."†

A difference so striking between the Constitutions of Great Britain and Ireland could not fail to awaken indignant observation. Mr. Yelverton, on giving notice that he would move for leave to introduce the heads of a bill, which was subsequently passed, for the modification of Poynings' Law,

---

* Lecky's "England in the Eighteenth Century," vol. iv. p. 358.
† Mountmorres's "Irish Parliament," vol. i. pp. 58, 59.

said that "at present our Constitution was the
Constitution of England inverted; bills originated
with the British Minister, and with this House it
only remained to register or reject them. This was a
miserable state of Ireland, and in this state it would
remain as long as a monster unknown to the Constitution—a British Attorney-General, through the
influence of the law of Poynings, had power to alter
our bills."*

Mr. Flood, who once stated that he had made
this particular question "his consideration for twenty
years,"† was of opinion that a construction had been
given to Poynings' Law, of which, when honestly regarded, it was incapable. "It was never intended," he
said, "by Poynings' Law to take away the right of Parliament, but merely to prevent the governors of Ireland
from giving the royal assent to laws that might be
injurious to the King. That during the civil wars of
York and Lancaster this had frequently happened.
That the adherents of the York family were numerous in Ireland, having been planted here chiefly
in the reign of Henry VI., who sent the Duke of
York with great power and great revenue to govern
this kingdom for no less than ten years, during which
time and afterwards it became an asylum to the
partisans of that house. That Lord Gormanstown,
who preceded Poynings, had given great cause for
suspicion—nay, it was even thought that when

---

* "Irish Debates," vol. i. p. 15.
† "Irish Debates," vol. i. pp. 185, 186.

Symnel was crowned in Dublin if there had been a Parliament sitting, that Parliament would have acknowledged him as rightful king. The voyages between England and Ireland in those days were much less frequent than between Europe and America at present, consequently many things happened here that were not known till long after in England, for which reason Henry VII., who derived his right from the House of Lancaster, when he chose that trusty servant Poynings to be his deputy here, though he had the utmost reliance on his fidelity, yet would not entrust even him with the power of giving the royal assent to laws till they had been notified to the King himself in England under the sanction of the Great Seal of Ireland ; but that this was considered only as a restraint on the governor, not on the Parliament of Ireland, which by many authentic records he proved had been in the constant practice of originating such bills as they thought proper, and sending them engrossed on parchment, sometimes through the Viceroy, sometimes by special messengers of their own, to receive the royal assent.

" He also produced the evidence of the Parliamentary Roll in the reign of Elizabeth to confirm this opinion, and to show the sentiments the Parliament then entertained of the law of Poynings by the reluctance with which they consented to a temporary suspension of its effects in favour of Lord Sydney, and the great compliment they paid that nobleman in the words of that consent. From this he inferred that Parliament had considered this as a popular law guarding the nation against evil governors, but in no wise restraining the power of either House of Parliament. He said that a very unjust stigma had therefore been cast on the name of Poynings, who was an able and upright governor, and from whose administration the kingdom had derived the greatest advantages, and whose laws were intended for its defence till prevented by the corrupt opinions of the judges. But he thought it no wonder that the people should receive an ill impression of the law of Poynings, as the very text of that law had been falsified by those who had charge of its publication, for instead of saying that the Imperial Crown of Ireland was inseparably annexed and appendent to the Imperial Crown of England, they had used the words dependent on, the most invidious perversion that could possibly be introduced. He said that Lord Bacon, who wrote the history of Henry VII., and who particularly mentions Poynings, would not have let so great a matter as a total inversion of our Constitution pass by the accuracy of his penetrating genius. He mentions the law of Poynings, indeed, but not this law. Speaking of Poynings, he says, 'But in Parliament he did endeavour to make amends for the meagreness of his service in the war, for there was that memorable Act called Poynings' Act (not the Act we are debating on), but that whereby all the Statutes of England were to be made of force in Ireland, for before (says Lord Bacon) *they were not.*

Neither are any now that were made in England since.'

"But," continued Mr. Flood, "it is astonishing that the law of Poynings should have received such a false and vicious interpretation as it now bears. Do we understand its meaning at the distance of almost three hundred years better than the people in whose days it was passed, or they who succeeded for an hundred years after? By them it was considered as a boon and a favour, but its operation now destroys the Constitution of Ireland, that Constitution which, growing on the same stem with the Constitution of Britain, it was formed to protect. But the law, he said, was not in fault, it was only the vile interpreter was to blame, an interpreter placed between the king and the people, a monster unknown to the Constitution, whose office was to stifle the voice of the people, and to prevent the king from hearing, to render the people dumb and the king deaf." *

The contrast between the Irish Constitution under Poynings' Act and the British Constitution has been frequently drawn, but by none more lucidly than by Molyneux in his "Case of Ireland," and by a Mr. Walshe in a speech delivered in the Irish House of Commons in the course of the same debate, in which Mr. Flood made the observations I have quoted. "By the Constitution of Ireland under Poynings' Act," says Molyneux, "the king's prerogative in the legislature is advanced to a much higher pitch than ever was chal-

* "Irish Debates," vol. i. 149—153, abridged.

lenged by the kings in England, and the Parliament of
Ireland stands almost on the same bottom as the king
does in England.   I say almost on the same bottom, for
the Irish Parliament have not only a negative vote (as
the king has in England) to whatever laws the king or his
Privy Councils of both or either kingdom shall lay before
them, but have also a liberty of proposing to the king
and his Privy Council here such laws as the Parliament
of Ireland think expedient to be passed.   Which laws,
being thus proposed to the king, and put into form,
and transmitted to the Parliament here, according to
Poynings' Act must be passed or rejected in the very
words even to a tittle, as they are laid before our Parliament, we cannot alter the least iota.   If, therefore,
the legislature of Ireland stand on this foot in relation
to the king and the Parliament of Ireland, and the
Parliament of England do remove it from this bottom,
and assume it to themselves, where the king's prerogative is much narrower, and as it were reversed (for
there the king has only a negative vote), I humbly con-
ceive it is an encroachment on the king's prerogative."*

Mr. Walshe, in the Irish House of Commons, thus
commented on the differences between the English and
the Irish Constitutions.   " By the English Constitution
the laws originate with the people—he meant with
either House of Parliament.   In England the people
suggest the laws they are willing to live under.   Can
there be a clearer idea of liberty?   In England the
only power the Crown has in legislation is that of

* "Case of Ireland," p. 113.

simply giving or refusing its assent. Neither the executive magistrate nor his council can alter a single sentence, nay, a single syllable, of the Bills offered to him by the people. His power is solely that of accepting or rejecting them *in toto*. Can the wisdom of the English Constitution appear in a clearer light than in this very instance—that of placing the power of originating laws in that very body of men that must necessarily be best acquainted with the grievances of the people, and must consequently best know what laws would be most salutary and conduce most to public good? The Constitution of Ireland was the very reverse of that of England. He was bold to say that it was the most extraordinary, the most preposterous Constitution that ever an independent people succumbed to. In Ireland the laws neither originated with the people nor directly with the Prince. In Ireland the laws originated with the Privy Council—a body unknown to and unconnected with the people— a body whose existence hung tremulous on the breath of Majesty. These men, generated in the sunshine of the Court, were to originate laws for Ireland in exclusion of the people. For by the 10th Hen. VII., c. 4, called Poynings' Law, it is enacted that no Parliament shall hereafter be holden in Ireland but at such season as the King's Lieutenant and Council of Ireland do first certify the King, under the Great Seal of Ireland, the causes and considerations and all such Acts as to them seemeth should pass in the same Parliament."

"The 3rd & 4th Philip & Mary. c. 4, which

D

expounds Poynings' Law, still increases the power
of the Privy Council, for by Poynings' Law the Privy
Council could only certify such causes and considerations and all such Acts as then seemeth should
pass previous to the meeting of Parliament.   That is,
the Privy Council must have pre-conceived all such
laws as they chose should pass, and must have certified them to England before the Parliament was convened, for Poynings' Law did not empower the Privy
Council to certify any causes or considerations after
Parliament had once met ; and therefore to increase
the power of the Privy Council was the Statute 3 & 4
Philip & Mary made, and that Statute enacts that
during the sitting of the Parliament the Lord-Lieutenant and the Privy Council shall and may certify
all such other causes and considerations as they shall
further think good to be enacted in the same Parliament, and such causes and considerations as shall be
thus certified and returned under the Great Seal of
Great Britain, and no others shall and may pass or be
enacted in the same Parliament—so that by these
two Statutes the Privy Council (a body elected by
the executive magistrate) are expressly appointed to
originate laws for Ireland in exclusion of her own
representatives.

"The introduction of heads of Bills into that House
so far as they could be said to originate laws before
they had been first certified to England was, he relied
on it, expressly and directly contrary to both the letter
and spirit of 10th Hen. VII., and 3 & 4 Ph. & M."

"The introduction of heads of Bills in their present situation was an absolute absurdity, was a mockery of reason and common sense, while there remained a power in the Privy Council to alter, to mutilate, nay, totally to suppress those Bills."

"There is a real abuse of those laws, there is a power usurped, not warranted by even the shadow of any law whatever—he meant the power usurped by the English Attorney-General. For," said he, "if the Privy Council should transmit bills unaltered into England, then they are to undergo the fiery ordeal of an English Attorney-General, of any man who fortuitously for the instant becomes the English Attorney-General, possibly as ignorant of the common rules of grammar as he is of the rights of Ireland. This man, buoyed up by the importance of office, thinks it his duty also to alter our bills ; he erases, he inserts, he expunges, for the sole purpose of stamping the Constitution of Ireland with the fiat of contempt. Thus we are reduced to this unhappy dilemma—either to adopt this man's blunders, or to reject the bill *in toto*. For by Poynings' Law we cannot alter a word in it. While Poynings' Law remains unmodified, the King of Ireland may know the wishes of his Lord-Lieutenant and Privy Council, but he cannot certainly know the sincere wishes of his people of Ireland. By Poynings' Law the Lord-Lieutenant and Privy Council have at this day a power to stop all communications between the King of Ireland and the Irish Parliament, a power the most extravagant, a power the most tyrannical that ever was obtruded on an independent people." *

The usual apology for the existence of arbitrary power, its general non-user, could not be urged in defence of this statute. The most casual glance at the history of the laws of the Irish Constitution will afford ample evidence of the persistent and reckless manner in which the provisions of Poynings' Law were called in aid to pervert, mutilate, suppress, and persecute every measure extending the benefits of the English Constitution to Ireland.

Poynings' Law was found so useful to the English Government in Ireland, that it is not surprising that efforts were made to extend its benefits. In 1678 a measure was introduced into the Legislative Assembly of Jamaica, embodying the main provisions of Poynings' Law. Two-thirds of the settlers of Jamaica were Irish by birth or by descent, which may account for the rejection of the proposal.†

---

* " Irish Debates," vol. i. pp. 162—167. Abridged.

† "In Charles II.'s time," says Mr. Long, "the Earl of Carlisle was sent here (to Jamaica) as Governor, and brought with him a body of laws fashioned after those in Ireland, pursuant to Poynings' Act, with instructions to get them passed here. But the Assembly rejected them with indignation ; no threats could frighten, no bribes could corrupt, no art nor arguments could persuade them to consent to laws that would enslave their posterity." Long's "History of Jamaica," vol. i. p. 11. See also *Ibid*, vol. i. pp. 15, 197—208. Sir G. C. Lewis refers to this transaction in his "Essay on Government of Dependencies, p. 156."

CHAPTER VI.

THE RELATION OF THE IRISH PARLIAMENT TO THE ENGLISH PRIVY COUNCIL AFTER 1782.

POYNINGS' ACT was not repealed by the revolution of 1782; it was merely modified. By the provisions of Yelverton's Act effecting this modification, no bills were to be originated, or altered, or suppressed by either Privy Council; but before any bill passed by both Houses of the Irish Parliament should receive the assent of the Lord-Lieutenant, as the King's representative, the consent of the Sovereign under the Great Seal of England was necessary. The clause, likewise, of Poynings' Act which rendered the Royal license to the Viceroy a condition precedent to the convening of a Parliament in Ireland was expressly retained.* The provisions of Yelverton's Act were framed in accordance with the terms of the Address to the Throne moved by Mr. Grattan on the 16th April, 1782, which contains the following passage :—
"To assure his Majesty that his Majesty's Commons in Ireland do most sincerely wish that all bills which become law in Ireland should receive the approbation of his Majesty under the Great Seal of Great Britain, but that yet we consider the practice of suppressing our bills in the Council of Ireland, or altering the

* 21 & 22 Geo. III., Ir. c. 47.

same anywhere, to be a just cause of jealousy and discontent." *

"At present," says Lord Mountmorres, writing in 1792, "by the Chief Baron Yelverton's law, it is not necessary for the Council to certify a bill under the Great Seal of Ireland as a reason for summoning a Parliament, but it is ordered to be convoked by proclamation from the Crown, as it is summoned in England. Touching bills, they now originate in either House, and go from one to the other, as they do in England, after which they are deposited in the Lords' office, when the clerk of the Crown takes a copy of them, and this parchment is attested to be a true copy by the Great Seal of Ireland on the left side of the instrument. Thus they are sent to England by the Irish Council, and if they are approved of by the King, this transmiss, or copy, comes back, with the Great Seal of England on the right side, with a commission to the Lord-Lieutenant to give the Royal assent. All bills, except money bills, remain in the Lords' office, but bills of supply are sent back to the House of Commons to be presented by the Speaker at the bar of the Lords for the Royal assent. Hence it is manifest that no alteration can now be made in bills, except in Parliament, as the record, or original bill, remains in the Lords' offices till it obtains the Royal assent." †

The nature and effects of this modification of Poynings' Law were discussed and explained in the

---

* "Irish Debates," vol. i. p. 337.
† Mountmorres's "Irish Parliament," vol. i. pp. 59, 60.

Irish Parliament during the debates on the Regency question. The distinction between the British and the Irish Constitution of 1782 in legislative procedure was then forcibly illustrated.

"By your new law," says Fitzgibbon, who was at that time Attorney-General, "you enact that all bills which pass the two Houses here which shall be certified into England, and which shall be returned under the Great Seal of England without any addition, diminution, or alteration whatever, shall pass into law, and no other. By this you make the Great Seal of England essentially and indispensably necessary on the passing of laws in Ireland. You can pass no act without first certifying it into England and having it returned under the Great Seal of that Kingdom, insomuch that were the King of England and Ireland to come here in person and to reside, he could not pass a bill without its being first certified to his regent in England, who must return it under the Seal of that Kingdom before his Majesty could even in person assent to it." "By this bill the Great Seal of England is the organ by which the King of England speaks, and the Great Seal of Ireland is the organ by which the King of Ireland speaks, and it is nonsense to say that it is as King of Ireland he affixes the Great Seal of England to Irish Acts. As well might you say that it is as King of Ireland he affixes the Great Seal of England to treaties of peace, alliance, and commerce, which nevertheless include Ireland."*

* "Irish Debates," vol. ix. pp. 48, 49.

To part of this statement Grattan took exception. "The bills," he said, "must return to this country; they must return without alteration, they must return under the Great Seal of Great Britain as usual, and then, says the right hon. gentleman (Fitzgibbon), they are the law. But I tell him they are not the law; they are then qualified to receive the royal assent, without which they cannot be law. That royal assent is the assent of the King of Ireland."*

"To every bill," said Hely Hutchinson, "in this kingdom, besides the assent of the two Houses, three things were necessary—the Great Seal of Ireland and the Great Seal of England, which must be affixed to every bill before it can pass into a law; but a third requisite was indispensable, namely, a commission for giving the royal assent." †

"Our Legislative Constitution," said Sir L. Parsons, "was altered in 1782, but the effects of these alterations have not as yet been fully considered. As it now stands, it agrees with the Legislative Constitution of England in having three estates—a King who acts by his Viceroy, a House of Lords, and a House of Commons; but it differs in this, that there is super-added upon our Constitution an extrinsic form which is distinct and independent of the three estates, and that is the Great Seal of England, which must be put to our bills before they become the law of the land. This is not the third estate, as some have called it, nor

* "Irish Debates," vol. ix. pp. 74, 75.
† "Irish Debates," vol. ix. p. 55.

do I think it can properly be called any estate at all ; if it be one, it must be a fourth estate." " It gives the English Parliament a kind of negative upon our laws, but by such a remote and severe action, as there is no reason to apprehend it will ever be abused. That Parliament having recognised our right to legislate exclusively for this kingdom, their own law as well as their prudence would not suffer them to impeach their Chancellor for putting that Seal to any Irish Act, except in the single case of its tending to destroy the unity of the executive power in which alone the connection of these kingdoms consists. The Seal, then, however it came to be added to our Constitution, whether by accident or design, is security to England without being dependent to Ireland ; and the history of mankind does not afford an instance of two independent States being connected together by a mechanism so wise and so beautiful." *

This exposition of the relation of the English king to the Irish Parliament between 1782 and 1800 is, in my judgment, accurate. The power of the veto, though it was not exercised, must, I think, be considered a real power, capable of use in emergencies. We can never sufficiently realise the great fact that the British Constitution is subject to constant changes. The power of the Crown a century ago cannot be ascertained by any estimate of the power of the Crown to-day. Mr. Bagehot stated the case strongly, but without exaggeration, when, in

* " Irish Debates," vol. ix. pp. 121, 122.

1865, he wrote: "The Queen has no veto; she must sign her own death-warrant if the two Houses unanimously send it up to her. It is a fiction of the past to ascribe to her legislative power. She has long ceased to have any."[*] In 1782 the royal veto on English legislation was not thought to be in abeyance, though it had not been exercised since 1693.[†] This position is proved by the fact that in the American Constitution, framed in 1789, which is a version of the English Constitution, the President, who supplies the place of the English king, has a modified veto in legislation.[‡] Still less could the veto on Irish legislation be considered as a nullity by statesmen who were accustomed, previously to 1782, to see bills suppressed, varied, and mutilated both by the Irish and the English Privy Council. So real did Flood, the greatest authority of his time on constitutional questions, consider the power of the royal veto under the new Constitution, that he urged the propriety of a provision requiring the royal dissent, as well as the royal assent, to be given in open Parliament. "Will you not," he said, "restore the Constitution to what it was

---

[*] "English Constitution," p. 57.

[†] When William III. refused his assent to the Bill for Triennial Parliaments which, notwithstanding, became law the following year. This is generally cited as the last instance of the exercise of the royal veto. The last actual instance, however, occurred in 1707, when Queen Anne refused her assent to a Scottish Militia Bill. But this is not regarded as a constitutional precedent.

[‡] See a very able article in the *Quarterly Review* for January, 1884, on the "Constitution of the United States."

before Poynings' Law? and every one knows that before Poynings' Law your bills were transmitted to the king engrossed on parchment, under the Great Seal of Ireland, and that the royal assent or dissent was given to them in open Parliament."*

"The power of the English Privy Council was not," says Mr. Butt, "regarded as a mere speculative or theoretical one. It was looked to as a practical check on Irish legislation. It is said—it is to be hoped not truly—that in 1792 the unanimity of the Irish House of Commons in favour of the Catholic Relief Bill was produced by the belief universally entertained that the English Privy Council would refuse their assent, and that the English Ministry returned it in spite, to punish the Irish Parliament for attempting to acquire a character for liberality at their expense. The story has probably as much foundation as most stories of the kind ; but its currency is sufficient to prove the opinions entertained of the reality of the veto." †

* "Irish Debates," vol. i. p. 392.
† "Irish Federation," pp. 40, 41.

CHAPTER VII.

THE IRISH ADMINISTRATION.

AN eminent political writer has described the English cabinet as "a board of control chosen by the Legislature out of persons whom it trusts and knows, to rule the nation." * This sentence is valuable, for it will impress on the mind by way of contrast the main characteristics of the Irish executive. The Irish Government in the interval between 1782 and 1800 consisted practically of the Lord-Lieutenant and his secretary. They were not chosen by the Irish Legislature, but by the English Government, whose creatures they were, and whose policy they came to Ireland to maintain. They were not generally known by the Irish Legislature before their acceptance of office, and when they became known they were for good reasons certainly not trusted. The Lord-Lieutenant was an English nobleman ; his secretary was generally a member of the English House of Commons, who easily obtained a seat in the Irish House. These functionaries went in and out of office with the English Government, whose nominees they were. In Ireland there was no Irish administration responsible to the Irish Parliament, and through that Parliament to the Irish nation. An adverse vote of the Parliament disturbed them not. Thus the

* Bagehot, " English Constitution," p. 13.

House of Commons in 1789 passed a vote of gravest censure on Lord Buckingham when Lord-Lieutenant, but he retained his office.* Lord Castlereagh's first proposal to the Irish Parliament on the question of Union miscarried, an amendment in favour of an independent legislature being lost by a single vote.† A virtual defeat on a leading question of policy would, in accordance with constitutional practice, have entailed the resignation of the Ministry, and the acceptance of office by a statesman opposed to the Union. But the Irish Ministers, looking for support not to Ireland but to England, recognised no such principle of action. They knew an easier plan. "It was plain," says Sir Erskine May, "that corrupt interests could only be overcome by corruption. Nomination boroughs must be bought, and their members indemnified, country interests conciliated, officers and expectant lawyers compensated, opponents bribed. Lord Castlereagh estimated the cost of these expedients at a million and a half, and the price was forthcoming." ‡

Theoretically the Ministers were liable to impeach-

---

* "That His Excellency the Lord-Lieutenant's answer to both Houses of Parliament requesting him to transmit their address to His Royal Highness the Prince of Wales is ill-advised, contains an unwarranted and unconstitutional censure on the proceedings of both Houses of Parliament, and attempts to question the undoubted rights and privileges of the Lords Spiritual and Temporal and the Commons of Ireland." Carried—ayes, 115; noes, 83.—"Irish Debates," vol. ix., pp. 153-155.

† May's "Constitutional History," vol. iii. p. 330. "Cornwallis Correspondence," vol. iii. pp. 40—51.

‡ "Constitutional History," vol. iii. p. 330.

ment for acts of administrative misconduct.* But this
cumbrous and unsatisfactory mode of procedure, as
Sir F. Stephen terms it, was not practically available,
owing to the "fugacious character" of Irish administrations. The Lord-Lieutenant and his secretary had
only to retire to England and oust the jurisdiction.
England would not be likely to deliver up officials
whose offence was that they served her interests not
honestly, but too well, and Ireland could not make
such a demand without a compromise of her national
dignity.

The general aim of the Irish Ministers was, it
seems, to regain by the corruption of Parliament the
arbitrary power which England lost by the Revolution
of 1782. This design was early perceived. Speaking
in the House of Commons on March 20, 1784,
Dr. Browne, one of the members for Trinity College,
makes this observation : " We are no longer attacked
by the stern violence of prerogative, but a new and
more dangerous foe has arisen, a corrupt and all-
subduing influence which, with a silent but resistless
course, has overwhelmed the land, and borne down
every barrier of liberty and virtue."† " Those acqui-
sitions in 1782," says Sir L. Parsons, "which the
people thought would have brought good government,

---

* This power was in fact never exercised by the Irish Parliament.
Hely Hutchinson, in a speech of great learning, urged that Lord
Strangford should be proceeded against by impeachment and not by a
bill of pains and penalties. He stated the constitutional principles
which he minutely explained and illustrated. The speech is worthy of
perusal. "Irish Debates," vol. iii. pp. 187—195.

† "Irish Debates," vol. iii. p. 73.

have brought bad, and why? Because it has been the object of the English Ministers ever since to countervail what was obtained at that period, and substitute a surreptitious and clandestine influence for that open power which the English Legislature was then obliged to relinquish."* Mr. Thomas Conolly, who was at the time a member of the English Parliament, thus spoke in 1791 in the Irish House of Commons: "As there was no other course established by which a member could quit that House, he must wish to be called to its bar and expelled. The British House of Commons consisted of 558 members, 67 only of whom were placemen, and no pensioners could sit, nor placemen, unless originally chosen as such, or upon getting a place, or being re-chosen. In this House, consisting of 300 members, 110 were placemen or pensioners. They had adopted the whole power of the Privy Council before the repeal of Poynings' Law, and literally appeared to be determined not to let any law pass here that was not agreeable to the English minister or the English merchant, and that therefore he was seriously in earnest to be expelled from a society which he conceived to be acting in direct contradiction to the constitution and trade of that kingdom."†

Grattan complains of "the fatal hand of an Irish Cabinet legislating against Ireland to promote its own credit in the Court of Great Britain."‡ In 1797

* "Irish Debates," vol. x. p. 243.
† "Irish Debates," vol. xi. pp. 231, 232.
‡ "Irish Debates," vol. xii. p. 14.

he observed :—" The unconstitutional and abomin-able interference of the British minister in every de-partment of our Constitution, to the ruin of its inde-pendency, and to the destruction of morals, has been made, by the servants of Government, the test of con-nection, and the Constitution itself has been made the test of separation." Painfully sensible of the analogy, he makes, in the same speech, this significant remark, " By ministers it was said, at the time of the American War, let the Parliament give up the power of making law for America, and the minister will get it by bribing."* Mr. Fox, in the British House of Commons in 1797, said, in reference to Ireland :— " The advantages which the form of a free govern-ment seemed to promise have been counteracted by the influence of the Executive Government, and of the British Cabinet." †

The want of responsible government was bitterly deplored. Commenting on the conduct of Secretary Orde in reference to the Commercial Propositions, Mr. Flood said :—" He may defy the House—he who can prorogue or even dissolve the Parliament. He, indeed, must be very much afraid of their resentment. No, but he may be afraid of a mob—if a whole offended, injured nation may be called a mob—and then what is his resource ? Why, a packet, and then he is responsible. Where ? In Dover !" ‡

---

* "Irish Debates," vol. xvii. pp. 503, 504.
† March 26th, 1797, reported in "Irish Debates," vol. xvii. p. 212.
‡ "Irish Debates," vol. v. p. 312.

"We have," said Grattan, "no Irish Cabinet. In-dividuals may deprecate, may dissuade, but they cannot enforce their principles; there is no embodied authority in Ireland. Again, your Government con-stantly fluctuates; your viceroys change every day; men of different parties and different principles, faith-ful to private engagements but not bound to any uniform public system. Again, you have no decided responsibility in Ireland; the objects of your inquest might not be easily found ; in short, you have in this country the misfortune of a double administration, a double importunity—a fluctuating Government, and a fugacious responsibility." * Some years later Mr. Grattan says, "Are the Ministers of Ireland fonder of the people of this country than the Ministers of the sister country are of Great Britain? Are they not often aliens in affection as well as birth, disposed to dispute your rights, censure your proceedings, and to boast that you cannot punish them, and that, therefore, they do not fear you? Are they not proud to humble you and ambitious to corrupt you ?" †

"There is in England," says Mr. Grattan in another debate, "such a thing as responsibility ; the public malefactor there cannot always retire from public mischief to triumphant impunity."‡ "We have been taught to believe the Irish Viceroy is not to be

* "Irish Debates," vol. vi. p. 115.
† "Irish Debates," vol. ix. p. 384.
‡ "Irish Debates, vol. x. pp. 59, 60

E

affected in his situation by the sense of the people of this country. The English Minister stands in a different situation with respect to his own." * " You have no adequate responsibility in Ireland, and politicians laugh at the sword of justice which falls short of their heads and only precipitates on their reputations. Sir, this country has never yet exercised herself in the way of vindictive justice ; in the case of Strafford she was but an humble assistant, and yet in this country we have had victims ; the aristocracy at different times has been a victim ; the whole people of Ireland for almost an entire century were a victim, but Ministers in all the criminal successions —— Here is a chasm, a blank in your history. Sir, you have in Ireland no axe, and therefore no good Minister." †

In his speech in the debate on the sale of the peerages, Mr. Grattan says :—" Some past administrations in this country prove that the most licentious thing imaginable is a little Castle presuming on the languor of the Empire, too low to think itself responsible to character, and too shifting to be responsible to justice. Remove from that Court the dread of Parliament, and they will become a political High Life Below Stairs, carrying not only the fashions but the vices and insolence of their superiors to outrageous excess." ‡

* " Irish Debates," vol. x. p. 61.
† " Irish Debates," vol. x. p. 67.
‡ " Irish Debates," vol. x. p. 267.

"I'll suppose," said Mr. Grattan, in the debate on the Responsibility Bill, in 1791, "the Commons of Ireland resolve articles of impeachment against a Chief Governor, and that they send their messengers to the Lords to acquaint them therewith, and to desire that he may be committed to their power. Where is he? He is fled. Fled with his secretary. Your impeachment would commence when his commission ceased, and his person was out of the jurisdiction of the realm. You can't follow his person nor find his property. These great men who are held out as our sole security for acts of State have seldom a freehold in your country. They could not be private, still less are they public security. I'll suppose on the application of this Parliament to his Majesty to interpose with the Parliament of Great Britain, the latter would transmit the person to be impeached ; but the efficacy of your jurisdiction depends on the success of your application ; that is, the responsibility held out to this country depends on the permission of the Parliament of another, which is in fact no responsibility whatever, and if ever the punishment of an unworthy Viceroy should become the unworthy cause of discontent and jealousy between the two countries, remember it is the servants of the Crown who are the cause, by leaving you no option and affording you no person whomsoever to proceed against, save only the person of the Viceroy. It follows from this that his Excellency affords no adequate responsibility. You can't derogate from your dignity and impeach him before the

Lords of England, nor attach his person when you impeach him before the Lords of Ireland." *

" The prominent spring of your Government, that is the British Minister, is an absentee, and does not look in the face the crimes committed by his agents in the kingdom of Ireland. Residence is a kind of physical responsibility, but he has the advantage of not beholding the acts of his servants in Ireland." "The agents, or instruments, in Ireland, by which these things are done, though they are not, like him, absentees, yet they are not stationary, and they look not only to the protection, but to the opinion of another country. The seat of their action is in Ireland; but the seat of their character, as well as of their punishment, is in England; and Ireland is, of course, deprived, in the present administration of her affairs, of the two great sanctions held necessary to restrain the malignity of human actions—the law of punishment, and the law of reputation; and the public weal of this country is left for its preservation to the remote apprehension which her ministers may entertain of Divine vengeance, and to their ambiguous speculations on a future state of reward and punishment."†

---

* "Irish Debates," vol. xi. p. 393.

† "Irish Debates," vol. xi. pp. 396, 397. A Responsibility Bill became law in 1793, but the position of the Lord-Lieutenant and his Secretary was not thereby changed. Throughout the whole existence of the Irish Parliament, these officials were practically beyond its control.

CHAPTER VIII.

POINTS OF DIFFERENCE BETWEEN THE LAWS AND PRACTICE OF THE ENGLISH AND THE IRISH CONSTITUTIONS.

By one of the articles of Poynings' Law, all statutes made in England prior to the passing of that Act are deemed valid in Ireland ; but as this provision did not extend to English statutes of later date, " the law of the countries began to diverge from that time, and, after three centuries has been in several respects differently modified." *

The chief points of difference between the British and the Irish Constitutions have been rendered apparent by the foregoing sketch, which, necessarily imperfect, would be still more incomplete without some further account of the distinctions in the practice and laws of the Constitutions of Great Britain and Ireland. The student of Irish Constitutional history will perceive that the beneficial Acts which are the essential preservations of the British Constitution, and the fundamental laws of that country, were, in some instances, not extended to Ireland for centuries after their enactment in England ; in other

* Hallam's " Constitutional History," vol. iii. p. 362.

cases, that they were extended, but after long intervals and in a mutilated form; while other statutes of equal importance were never extended to Ireland at all.

The reason of so striking a phenomenon is quite apparent. Before 1782 the friends of popular rights in Ireland had to cope with the Irish and English Privy Council armed with the machinery provided by Poynings' Law for the destruction of constitutional liberty. After 1782 they had to struggle against the influence of an Irish Ministry who were the agents of the English Cabinet for the bribery of a Parliament, unreformed, and from its very nature subject to corruption. If we take into consideration the constitution of that assembly, the tendencies of the time, the want of an independent newspaper press, the low state of public opinion, and the temptations by which political rectitude was assailed, so far from agreeing with Mr. Froude that the Irish Parliament was "the most mischievous parody of a representative legislature which the world has ever seen," * we shall be led insensibly to admire a body who gained for their country many of the benefits of the British constitution, despite the determined opposition of a ministry enforced by unlimited means of corruption. "A person of high consideration," said Fox in the British House of Commons, "was known to say that £500,000 had been expended to quell an opposition in Ireland, and that as much more must be expended

* Froude's "English in Ireland," vol. iii. p. 551.

to bring the legislature of that country into a proper temper." *

The following are some of the leading differences in the practice and laws of the Constitution in Great Britain and Ireland :—

1. *Laws regulating the duration and convening of Parliament.*

In England, previous to 1694, the old maxim prevailed that the king is *caput principium et finis* of Parliament. The House of Commons accordingly, unless dissolved, remained in existence during the life of the monarch who convened it. A Triennial Act had indeed been passed by the Long Parliament; it was, however, violated by that assembly, and repealed at the Restoration. In 1693 a Triennial Bill was passed by both the English Houses of Parliament, and presented to William III., who refused his assent. This measure, however, became law in the following year. In 1715 the Septennial Act was passed, since a general election at the time was considered perilous to the existence of the Hanoverian dynasty. This statute has since remained in force, though many efforts have been made to obtain a return to the old system of Triennial Parliaments. By a statute of Anne it is provided that Parliament, if not sooner dissolved by the new sovereign, should remain in existence for six months after a demise of the Crown, while a statute

* "Irish Debates," vol. xvii. p. 212. British House of Commons, March 26th, 1796. The reference was to Fitzgibbon, who, when Attorney-General, made use of this observation in the House of Commons.

of George III. enacts that if a demise of the Crown should take place at a time when no Parliament is in existence, the last Parliament should revive and continue in being, unless again dissolved, for six months. The Reform Act of 1867 provides that the demise of the Crown shall have no effect on the existence of Parliament.

In Ireland, previous to 1768, Parliament, unless dissolved, lasted during an entire reign. This had actually occurred; the Parliament of George II. remained in existence during his whole reign, a period of thirty-three years. Flood entered this assembly in 1759 at the mature age of seven-and-twenty; he was, however, some years younger than the Parliament. The Irish House of Commons had frequently passed the heads of Septennial Bills, which had been forwarded to England but never returned. In 1768 a Septennial Bill was returned by the Privy Council altered into an Octennial Bill, in the hope, as it has been asserted, that the Irish Parliament would not accept it thus changed. They, however, gladly passed the measure in its mutilated form. The grounds for the alteration by the English Privy Council were alleged to be the fact that the Irish Parliament sat only every second year, and that great inconvenience would arise if both England and Ireland were plunged at the same time in the turmoil of a general election.

The effects of the Octennial Act cannot be over-estimated. "Our sovereign," said Mr. R. H. Hutchinson, in the House of Commons, in 1781, "has given a perpetual spring to our national spirit by lopping off that branch of his prerogative which enabled him to make the representatives of the people free-holders of their trust." *   "The enactment of that law produced," said Mr. Fletcher, "a revolution more salutary than the boasted Revolution of 1688." †   Mr. Lecky considers this Act to have "laid the foundation of Parliamentary influence and independence in Ireland." ‡

The contrast between an English House of Commons, elected for three years, extending its tenure to seven years, and an Irish House of Commons, elected for the life or during the pleasure of the sovereign, wishing to limit its tenure of office to seven years, is noteworthy.

As regards the convening of Parliament in England, a statute of Edward II. and two statutes of Edward III. provide that "a Parliament shall be held once annually, or more often if need be."   These Acts are considered to refer merely to the meeting of Parliament, and not to the summoning of a new Parliament. They were, however, frequently violated.   Charles I., for instance, allowed twelve years to elapse without summoning a Parliament.   Again, the Bill of Rights declares that Parliaments ought to be held more frequently.   From the Revolution, owing to the

* "Irish Debates," vol. i. p. 269.
† "Irish Debates," vol. xv. p. 323.
‡ "England in the Eighteenth Century," vol. iv. p. 382.

necessity of passing the annual Mutiny Act and the Appropriation Act, Parliament in England has met once a year.

These statutes of Edward II. and Edward III. were of course in operation in Ireland under Poynings' Law; their provisions were, however, disregarded more flagrantly in Ireland than in England. "Of the seventeenth century," says Grattan, "nearly 85 years at different intervals passed without a Parliament: from 1585 to 1612, that is 27 years, no Parliament; from 1615 to 1634, 19 years, no Parliament; from 1648 to 1661, 13 years, no Parliament; from 1666 till 1692, that is 26 years, no Parliament. Before the Revolution, it thus appears that, with the rights and name, Ireland had not the possession of a Parliamentary constitution; and it will appear that, since the Revolution, she had no constitutional Parliament. From 1692 till 1768, near 70 years, almost two-thirds of a century, the tenure was during the life of the king."

Ireland never had a Bill of Rights. In the first Parliament that was held after the Revolution, the heads of a Bill containing the chief provisions of the Bill of Rights were sent to England. It was, however, never returned. From 1692 till 1782 Parliaments met biennially; from 1782 till 1800 there were annual sessions.

2. *The Mutiny Act.*—The first English Mutiny Act was passed in 1689. It was a temporary measure, framed for the purpose of suppressing a mutiny which

---

* "Irish Debates," vol. xiv. p. 84.

had broken out in some regiments under orders for foreign service.* It was found so conducive to military discipline that its provisions have been re-enacted every year, with the exception of a few years in William III.'s reign. The continuance of the Mutiny Act is limited to a year. It provides the sole means of enforcing military discipline and keeping the army together. It asserts the clause of the Bill of Rights, whereby the raising or keeping of a standing army within the kingdom in time of peace, except with the consent of Parliament, is declared to be against law, and it asserts that it is adjudged necessary by the Sovereign and by Parliament that a body of forces should be maintained for the safety of the kingdom, and that an exact discipline should be observed. After reciting the provisions of the Petition of Right, and of 31 Car. II., c. 1, against the billeting of soldiers, it suspends those provisions, and permits billeting in inns and victualling houses.

There was no Mutiny Act in Ireland previous to 1779. Discipline in the army was maintained, and prisoners were tried by court-martial, and punished, either under the provisions of the English Mutiny Act or under a prerogative of which it might be contended the Irish Crown had not been deprived. When the sentiment against the validity of English laws in Ireland became general, it was seen that no convictions could be obtained for offences against the English Mutiny Act.

* Macaulay's "History of England," vol. iii. pp. 45, 45.

Under these circumstances, the heads of an Annual Mutiny Bill, which were introduced into Parliament, passed the House of Commons. They were, however, returned from England with the limitation as to time expunged. The Parliament accepted the alteration, and thus a perpetual Mutiny Act passed, containing no assertion of the necessity of the assent of Parliament to the maintenance of an army in time of peace.* In 1782 this perpetual Mutiny Act was repealed, and from that time till the Union, a Mutiny Act was passed annually, framed on the model of the English Act, and containing the same provisions and recitals.

3. *The Habeas Corpus Act.*—The celebrated English statute known as the Habeas Corpus Act, was passed in 1679. Mr. Hallam observes that it is a common mistake to suppose "that this statute enlarged to a great degree our liberties, and forms a sort of epoch in their history. But though a very beneficent enactment, and eminently remedial in many cases of arbitrary imprisonment, it introduced no new principle, nor conferred any right upon the subject." "It was not to bestow an immunity from arbitrary imprisonment, which is abundantly provided in Magna Charta (if, indeed, it were not much more ancient), that the statute of Charles II. was enacted, but to cut off the abuses by which the Government's

---

* This measure was severely condemned by Edmund Burke ; he characterises it ''as the perpetual establishment of a military power in the dominions of this Crown without the consent of the British Legislature, contrary to the policy of the Constitution, contrary to the Declaration of Rights."—"Irish Affairs," pp. 130, 131.

lust of power, and the servile subtlety of Crown lawyers, had impaired so fundamental a privilege."*

The heads of the Bill extending the provisions of the Habeas Corpus Act to Ireland had again and again been transmitted to England but were never returned. Indeed, the Irish Privy Council had been told "to transmit the Bill no more." Such a Bill was, in the words of Lord Harcourt, when Lord-Lieutenant, in a letter written to Lord Rochford, dated March 6th, 1774, "held irreconcilable with the idea of a dependency." It was regarded as "a solecism in politics to make the constitution of a colony the same as that of the mother country." "The Catholics must be either admitted to the protection of it, or be excluded." The Viceroy then proceeds to state what seem to him the dangers either of admitting or excluding them—throwing on the English Council the onus of arriving at a decision.†

When, in 1781, the heads of a Habeas Corpus Bill were introduced, Mr. Eden, the Secretary, said "that from the usage of Ireland, which was the common law of the realm, and from the conduct of the Judges, the Habeas Corpus Act was in operation in Ireland, though not under the authority of Statute,"‡ but admitted that the rights of the subject should be secured by positive law. A Habeas Corpus Act was accordingly passed which, while differing in some

* See "Constitutional History," vol. iii. pp. 10—15.
† See Froude's "English in Ireland," vol. ii. pp. 178, 179.
‡ "Irish Debates," vol. i. p. 31.

unimportant particulars from the English statute,
contained a clause enabling the operation of the Act
to be suspended by the Lord-Lieutenant and Privy
Council, in the event of actual invasion or rebellion in
Great Britain or Ireland.*

4. *The Independence of the Judges.* — The Act
of Settlement provides that after the accession
of the House of Hanover the English Judges' commissions should be made during good behaviour,
and their salaries ascertained and established ; but
upon the address of both Houses of Parliament it
may be lawful to remove them. "William III.,"
says Mr. Hallam, "gave an unfortunate instance of
his very injudicious tenacity of bad prerogatives in
refusing his assent in 1692 to a Bill that had passed
both Houses for establishing this independence of
the judges by law, and confirming their salaries."†
From the first year of George I., however, English
judges have been independent.   The independence of
the Irish judges was not secured by a provision similar
to that contained in the Act of Settlement till 1782.
"English Ministers had," says Mr. Froude, "been peculiarly tenacious of their power to remove them (the
Irish judges) at will."‡   The heads of a Judges' Tenure
Bill had again and again been forwarded, but had not
been returned by the Privy Council.   The history of a
few of these Bills may perhaps, be given as showing

---

* 21 & 22 Geo. III., Ir., c. 11.
† "Constitutional History," vol. iii. p. 194.
‡ "English in Ireland," vol. ii. p. 59.

the species of opposition the extension to Ireland of any constitutional measure had to encounter. In 1767 Lord Townshend, then Viceroy, made mention, in a speech from the throne, that he had been instructed to recommend that provision should be made for securing the judges in their seats during good behaviour. For this he was sharply reprimanded by Lord Shelburne, inasmuch as he exceeded his instructions, which were merely to speak in private conversation, and in general terms, to influential politicians of the determination of the Government to support a Judges' Bill and other popular measures.* Immediately the heads of a Bill assimilating the tenure of the Irish judges to that of the English judges were passed in the House of Commons and transmitted to the Privy Council.

"The English Ministers," says Mr. Lecky, "were determined that the Irish Privy Council should be recognised as an essential part of the Irish Constitution, and that the dependence of Ireland on the English Parliament should be emphatically asserted. Shelburne wrote to Townshend that the Irish judges should be removable only upon a representation of the two Irish Houses of Parliament and the Irish Privy Council, conjointly or upon an address of the two Houses of the British Parliament. Townshend at once summoned the confidential servants of the Crown, and directed them to have clauses to this effect inserted in committee; but they all answered

* "English in Ireland," vol. ii. pp. 59, 60.

that such clauses would be rejected with indignation, and they entreated him to keep it secret that they had ever been thought of. The Bill was therefore suffered to proceed to England in a form corresponding with the English Act, but it was returned with clauses making it necessary for addresses of the two Irish Houses for the removal of a judge to be certified by the Privy Council, and making the Irish judges removable by the British Parliament. The Irish House of Commons at once rejected the Bill ; and the promise in the speech from the throne was branded, with some reason, as not* much better than a deception." *

Nine years afterwards (in 1776) Lord Harcourt, in transmitting the heads of a Judges' Tenure Bill, thus wrote to Lord Weymouth : — "The state of the country duly considered, I am persuaded it would be undesirable to make the commission of judges to continue during good behaviour. So many inconveniences would result from such a Bill that I trust it will not be deemed proper to return it to Ireland." †

Again, in 1780, on the rejection of the heads of a Judges' Tenure Bill by the English Privy Council, Lord Buckingham, the Lord Lieutenant of the day, thus writes :—" As the having the commissions of the Irish judges the same as in England, has been a favourite wish in this country, it was never, as I

* "England in the Eighteenth Century," vol. iv. pp. 374, 375. See "English in Ireland," vol. ii. pp. 59—68.
† " English in Ireland," vol. ii. pp. 200, 201.

understand, thought expedient to oppose the heads in the House of Commons, the reasons upon which these heads have been disapproved by his Majesty's British servants not being of a nature to be agitated here even in quiet times." *

In September, 1781, Lord Carlisle, then Viceroy, recommends the English Privy Council to pass this Bill. Lord Hillsborough thus replies: "As to giving the Irish judges the same position which the judges had in England . . . the King's servants had to observe that nothing could be more dangerous and improper than such an Act without the clauses which were inserted by the Privy Council in the former Bill, on which it was thrown out by the House of Commons in Ireland." †

One of the first Acts of the free Irish Parliament in 1782 was to secure an upright administration of the law, by giving the Irish judges the independence enjoyed by the English judges for a period of sixty-two years previously. ‡ In the eloquent words of Flood, "The Houses of Parliament were made guardians of the integrity of the Bench."§

5. *Money Bills.*—"The jealousy of the House of Commons in England at all periods to originate all grants of money and money bills, and to pass them

---

* Froude, "English in Ireland," vol. ii. p. 269.

† Froude, "English in Ireland," vol. ii. p. 315.

‡ 21 & 22 Geo. III., Ir., c. 50.

§ "Irish Debates," vol. v. p. 16. An English Statute passed in 1 Geo. III., provides that judges should continue in office, notwithstanding the demise of the Crown. The Irish Statute incorporates the provisions of this Statute and of the clause in the Act of Settlement.

F

unaltered by the Lords or Crown is," says Lord Chief
Justice Whiteside, "proverbial.   It has been carried
to a ridiculous extreme.*   From the ninth of
Henry IV. the principle has been recognised in
England that Money Bills must originate in the Lower
House.†   From the period of Charles I. the name of
the Lords has been omitted in the preamble of the
Bills of Supply, the Commons reciting the grant as if
wholly their own, but in the enacting words adopting
the customary form of statutes. ‡   In 1671 the Commons resolved, "That in all aids given to the King
by the Commons the rate or tax ought not to be
altered by the Lords." §   Since the Revolution they
have still further extended their privilege "by not
receiving from the House of Lords any Bill which
imposes a pecuniary penalty on offenders, nor per-
mitting them to alter the application of such as had
been imposed below." ‖   "Taxation," says Lord
Chatham, "is no part of the governing or legislative
power.   The taxes are a voluntary gift and grant of
the Commons alone.   In legislation the three estates
of the realm are alike concerned, but the concurrence
of the Peers and the Crown to a tax is only necessary
to clothe it with the form of a law.   The gift and
grant is of the Commons alone." ¶

---

* "Life and Death of the Irish Parliament," p. 110
† Hallam, "Middle Ages," vol. iii. p. 103.
‡ Hallam, "Constitutional History," vol. iii. p. 29.
§ Hallam, "Constitutional History," vol. iii. p. 30.
‖ Hallam, "Constitutional History," vol. iii. p. 32.
¶ May, "Constitutional History," vol. ii. p. 104.

In Ireland, before 1782, Bills were certified by the Privy Council in Ireland to the Privy Council in England as a reason for summoning a new Parliament. As if to accentuate in the most invidious manner the fact that the Irish House of Commons was deprived of privileges asserted and maintained by the English House, it was customary that one of these Bills should be a Bill of Supply.

In the very first Irish Parliament after the Revolution, of 1688, the Parliament of 1692,* two Money Bills were thus originated by the Privy Council. The House of Commons passed one to meet the exigencies of the Government. The other they rejected, alleging by a resolution " that it was and is the undoubted right of the Commons of Ireland in Parliament assembled to prepare and resolve the ways and means of raising money." The Viceroy, Lord Sidney,

---

* The first Parliament which actually sat after the Revolution of 1688 was the Parliament convened by James II., subsequently to his " abdication " of the throne. This Assembly cannot, from a constitutional point of view, be regarded as a legally convened Parliament. Mr. Lecky has, however, done much to rescue its memory from the avalanche of abuse with which a certain school of writers have overwhelmed it. Edmund Burke thus refers to this Parliament : " The Irish Parliament of 1782 bore little resemblance to that which sat in that kingdom after the period of the Revolution of 1688. It bore a much nearer resemblance to that which sat under King James. The change of the Parliament in 1782 from the character of the Parliament which, as a token of its indignation, had burned all the journals indiscriminately of the former Parliament, in the Council Chamber was very visible. The address of King William's Parliament—the Parliament which assembled after the Revolution—amongst other causes of complaint (many of them sufficiently just) complains of the repeal by their predecessors of Poynings' Law ; no absolute idol with the Parliament of 1782.' " Irish Affairs," p. 242.

prorogued and afterwards dissolved this Parliament, pronounced the vote of the Commons to be " contrary to the laws of their constitution," and required his protest to be entered on the journals.*

In 1760, at the accession of George III., the Lords Justices and the Irish Privy Council remonstrated on the practice of sending over Money Bills as a reason for summoning Parliament. The English Privy Council, however, insisted on a proceeding which the Irish Parliament regarded as a wanton invasion of their privileges.

The Money Bill was certified, and was on this occasion easily carried through Parliament—Gerard Hamilton, who was secretary to the Lord-Lieutenant, thus maintaining in the Irish House of Commons the right of another body to originate Money Bills. " As to the analogy between this and the British House of Commons, every argument must be inconclusive which means to assimilate things which are in their very form and origin—in their very first concoction —not only different, but opposite. The two Constitutions were once indeed on the same model." "The plan of Poynings' Act was to remove the Irish Constitution from the ground on which it stood— to change the model of it—and to make it not only different, but in some respects the very reverse of the English House of Commons." †

* Whiteside's " Life and Death of the Irish Parliament," pp. 111, 112. Froude's " English in Ireland," vol. ii. pp. 253, 254.

† Whiteside, " Life and Death of the Irish Parliament," p. 113. This speech is subjoined to a work of Gerard Hamilton's, entitled " Parliamentary Logick."

Money Bills, however, which were originated by the Privy Council were generally rejected, and their mere rejection was not resented ; for although the English Government claimed the right to originate Money Bills, the right of the Irish Parliament to reject them was not disputed. In 1769, however, the first Parliament that met after the Octennial Act threw out the Money Bill which had been certified by the Privy Council as the cause for summoning it, and passed a resolution stating that this Bill had been rejected "because it did not take its rise in the House of Commons."

This resolution was construed by the Government to be a denial of their right to originate Money Bills, Lord Townshend protested against it as an infringement of Poynings' Law, and prorogued Parliament.*

In the interval between 1782 and 1800 the Irish House of Commons exercised all the privileges of the English House of Commons with respect to Money Bills.

6. *The Law of Treason.*—In England, immediately after the Revolution of 1688, many important safeguards were provided by statutes for persons charged with the crime of high treason. Thus, the 7th William III. c. 3, enacts that every person who shall be accused and indicted under the 25th Edward III. shall have a true copy of the whole indictment delivered to him upon request five days at least before

* For full account of this transaction see "England in the Eighteenth Century," vol. iv. pp. 390—392.

he shall be tried for the same, to enable him to advise with counsel thereon to plead and make his defence. It also provides that so many counsel as the prisoner shall desire, not exceeding two, shall upon his request be assigned by the Court to plead for and assist him in making his defence ; that no person is to be tried or attainted of high treason but upon the oaths of two witnesses ; that there must be two witnesses to each distinct species of treason, and that the indictment must be found within three years after the offence. A statute of Anne * further provides that a list of jurors and witnesses, together with a copy of the indictment, shall be delivered to any party indicted for treason ten days before the trial.

These great provisions found no place in the Irish statute book. In 1765, indeed, by an Irish statute, the prisoner in cases of treason was accorded the privilege of a copy of the indictment and of having counsel assigned to aid him in his defence.† From the other securities afforded by these statutes to persons in peril on a charge of high treason in England a prisoner similarly situated in Ireland was excluded.

In the celebrated case of Sir John Fenwick, in the reign of William III., one of the two witnesses required by the law of England to substantiate a charge of treason was prevailed on by the wife of the accused to quit the kingdom. It became impossible, accord-

---

* 7 Anne, c. 21.
† 5 Geo. III. Ir., c. 21.

ingly, to obtain a conviction in the course of law. Resort was had to a Bill of Attainder, which became law, and under whose provisions Sir J. Fenwick suffered the penalties of high treason. "The jealous sense of liberty," says Mr. Hallam, "prevalent in William's reign, produced a very strong opposition to this Bill of Attainder." * The constitutional aspect of the question is to this hour a matter of animated discussion.

In Ireland, however, no such controversy could have arisen—the one witness who was forthcoming would have been abundantly sufficient to convict the prisoner in accordance with the ordinary rules of law.

On the 29th April, 1795—nearly a century after Sir J. Fenwick's attainder—Mr. Curran, from his place in the Irish House of Commons, moved for leave to bring in a Bill for amending the Irish laws in cases of high treason, in a speech, in the course of which "he alluded to the difference which was said to exist between the laws relative to high treason in this country and Great Britain, in the latter of which two witnesses were necessary in order to convict the accused, while in this country a single witness was deemed sufficient." †

Mr. Curran's Bill never became law. It was not till 1821 that the remaining provisions of the statute of William III.,‡ and not till 1854 that the pro-

---

* See Hallam, "Constitutional History," vol. iii. pp. 131—133.
† "Irish Debates," vol. xv. p. 200.
‡ 1 & 2 Geo. IV. c. 24.

visions of the statute of Anne were extended to Ireland.*

7. *Appropriation of Supplies.*—" The great and fundamental principle," says Mr. Hallam, " that the money voted by Parliament is appropriated, and can only be applied to certain specified heads of expenditure, was introduced (in England) in the reign of Charles II., and generally, though not in every instance, adopted by his Parliament. From the Revolution it has been the invariable usage. The Lords of the Treasury, by a clause annually repeated in the Appropriation Act of every session, are forbidden, under severe penalties, to order by their warrant any moneys in the Exchequer, so appropriated, from being issued for any other service, and the officers of the Exchequer to obey any such warrant. This has given the House of Commons so effectual a control over the executive power, or, more truly speaking, has rendered it so much a participator in that power, that no Administration can possibly subsist without its concurrence, nor can the session of Parliament be intermitted for an entire year without leaving both the naval and military force of the kingdom unprovided for." †

In Ireland the absence of such a provision was, in the year 1753, strikingly exemplified. Lord Chief Justice Whiteside thus relates this remarkable incident : " An amusing yet conclusive example of the

---

* 17 and 18 Vict., c. 26.
† Hallam, " Constitutional History," vol. iii. p. 117.

imbecility of our Senate is furnished by the result of
the memorable dispute between the Irish House of
Commons and Primate Stone, another intriguing
English prelate, then a Minister, and representing the
Irish Executive, as to the disposal of an unexpected
surplus of £200,000 in the Irish Treasury after all
charges on the public funds had been paid. The
Irish House of Commons insisted they had the right
to appropriate the money they had granted. The
local Executive replied that such a doctrine had never
before been heard of in Ireland. The dispute waxed
hot, meanwhile the money was drawn out by a king's
letter, and disposed of according to the pleasure of the
Crown, leaving the disputants to quarrel about the
shell when the oyster was gone." *

The advocates of constitutional liberty long un-
successfully endeavoured to assimilate the laws of the
two countries in this respect, and bitterly deplored
that so precious a right was withheld from Ireland.
" In Ireland," says George Ponsonby, "the revenues
are not appropriated ; in England they are. In Ireland the Crown draws what money it thinks proper
out of the Treasury in England ; it cannot apply a
shilling but to the purposes for which it is appropriated."† At length, in 1793, the Appropriation
Bill became law, the revenue of the country being
thereby vested in responsible commissioners.

---

* " Life and Death of the Irish Parliament," pp. 108—9. See Hallam's account of this transaction, "Constitutional History," vol. iii. p. 408.

† " Irish Debate ' vol. x. p. 386.

8. *Placemen and Pensioners in Parliament.*—It was provided by the Act of Settlement that no person who has an office or place of profit under the king, or receives a pension from the Crown, shall be capable of serving as a member of the House of Commons of England. This section was repealed by the 4th Anne, c. 8, before it came into operation. It is, however, of value to the student of constitutional law, as the fact of such a clause—which would exclude every Minister of the Crown from the House of Commons —having passed into law demonstrates the modern origin of our ministerial system. By the 6th Anne, c. 7, it is provided that every member of the House of Commons accepting an office under the Crown, except a higher commission in the army, must vacate his seat, but may be re-elected ; while persons holding offices created since the 25th October, 1705, are incapacitated from being elected or re-elected members of Parliament. It excludes those who hold pensions during the pleasure of the Crown, and enacts that no greater number of commissioners should be appointed to execute any office than had been employed in its execution at some time before that Parliament. By the Reform Act of 1867 members who may be removed from one office under the Crown to another are relieved from the ordeal of re-election.*

In Ireland many efforts were made to obtain a Place and Pension Bill similar to the English statute. The pensions charged on the Civil List were such

---

* 30 & 31 Vict., c. 102, s. 52, and sch. 4.

an intolerable grievance, that in 1757 the House of
Commons passed resolutions denouncing their increase, which they compelled the Lord-Lieutenant,
under threat of withholding the supplies, to forward
to the king. In 1763 the heads of a Bill, copied from
the English Place Act, were described as "very
popular. The increase of places and pensions, however, grew apace despite all the efforts of the country
party to check it."*

Mr. Grattan, in supporting Mr. Forbes's annual
Pension Bill, in 1789, which passed the House of
Commons that year, but was lost in the Lords, thus
spoke: "When gentlemen call this Bill an attack on
the prerogative of the Crown they are answered by
the principles of the Constitution; but they are
also answered by a precedent of a most decisive
nature, and that precedent is this very Bill which is
now the law of England. By the law of England
no pensioner for years or during pleasure can sit in
Parliament, and by the law of England the amount
of pensions is limited. The first law passed at the
time of the Revolution, and was improved in the
reign of Queen Anne. The latter passed in 1782,
with the entire concurrence of these very persons
who now constitute this Administration. Yet the
argument of prerogative would have been stronger
in England, because there a Civil List has been
granted to the king, and the subsequent limitation

* See Lecky's "England in the Eighteenth Century," vol. iv. pp.
365—367, 371.

of pensions in that list seemed a revocation of the powers of the grant. On what authority, then, or pretence do gentlemen call a measure which they supported as necessary for England, an invasion of the rights of the Crown when proposed for the benefit of Ireland ? What pretence have they for such a partial doctrine of unequal measure? As if that was an infringement in Ireland which in England was constitutional, or as if what was moderation in the people of England would be in those of Ireland arrogance and presumption."*

"In 1793 the Parliament of Ireland adopted the principles of the English Act of Anne, and disqualified the holders of all offices under the Crown and Lord-Lieutenant created after that time."†

Writing in 1792, a year before that enactment, Lord Mountmorres says, "Employments in Ireland do not vacate seats, and in England the Chiltern Hundreds appear to have been offices devised to carry a point by a manœuvre." ‡ After 1793 the Escheatership of Munster served a similar purpose for the members of the Irish Parliament. Before that time a seat in the Irish Parliament was vacated only in the following instances—by death, by being made a peer or a judge, or by taking holy orders. §

9. *Economic Reform.*—The year 1782 was signalised in England by Lord Rockingham's great

---

* "Irish Debates," vol. vi. p. 310.
† May's "Constitutional History," vol. i. p. 373.
‡ Mountmorres's "Irish Parliament," vol. ii. pp. 189, 190.
§ Mountmorres's "Irish Parliament," vol. ii. p. 8.

measure of economic reform which was the product of the genius of Edmund Burke.

"In Ireland the pension list, which in 1757 had amounted to £40,000 was trebled in the first thirty years of George III., and in 1793 had reached the prodigious sum of £124,000. But the abuse had now worked itself out, and could be tolerated no longer. In that year, therefore, the Government itself proposed a change which was readily adopted by the Irish Parliament. The hereditary revenues were surrendered to Ireland—as they had previously been surrendered in England—in exchange for a fixed civil list of £145,000, exclusive of pensions, and a pension list of £124,000, to be eventually reduced to £80,000. Meanwhile the Crown was restrained from granting pensions in any one year exceeding £1,200, but still retained and exercised the power of granting pensions for life and in reversion." *

10. *Laws affecting Religious Liberty.*—In 1778 the first Roman Catholic Relief Act was passed in England. The penalties which were then repealed were imposed in 1700. They were the perpetual imprisonment of priests for officiating in the services of their Church, the forfeiture of the estates of Roman Catholic heirs educated abroad in favour of the next Protestant heir, and the prohibition to acquire

* May, "Constitutional History," vol. i. pp. 259, 260. For a very clear and succinct account of the hereditary revenues of the Crown in Ireland, see speech of Hely Hutchinson, "Irish Debates," vol. xiii. pp. 476, 477. See also Lecky's "England in the Eighteenth Century," vol. ii. pp. 223, 224.

land by purchase. This Act, which passed unanimously through the Houses of Parliament, gave rise to the riots of 1780, which are associated with the name of Lord George Gordon. These disturbances postponed all measures for further relief of Roman Catholics till 1791, when the Roman Catholics in England on taking an oath not obnoxious to their general body, were secured complete freedom of worship and education, while their property was exempted from invidious regulations, the practice of the law opened to them in all its branches, and the ancient privilege of intercourse with the king restored. * When, however, in 1823 Lord Nugent sought to extend to English Catholics the elective franchise given to Irish Catholics by the Irish Parliament in 1793, the measures miscarried in the Lords, and, though repeatedly brought into Parliament, did not become law.† The elective franchise was not extended to Roman Catholics in England till 1829.

O'Connell thus described, in 1843, the efforts of the Irish Parliament in the cause of religious liberty, " But for the Union we should have been emancipated by our Protestant fellow-countrymen long before. In 1778 they restored the Catholics to the equal enjoyment of all property they then held, and enabled them to acquire long terms for years in lands. In 1782 the Irish Protestants restored the Catholics to the capacity of acquiring every species of freehold

---

* May's " Constitutional History," vol. iii. pp. 96—99, 106, 107.
† May's " Constitutional History," vol. iii. p. 151.

property, and to enjoy it equally with Protestants. In 1792 and 1793 the learned professions were to a certain extent opened to Catholics—the grand-jury box, the magistracy, partial rank in the army, were all conceded by the Irish Protestants to their Catholic fellow-countrymen. But, greatest of all, the elective franchise was restored. Under these circumstances, but for the Union, full and complete emancipation would have been conceded before 1803." *

* Discussion in Dublin Corporation on Repeal of the Union in 1843, p. 50.

THE END.

PRINTED BY CASSELL & COMPANY, LIMITED, LA BELLE SAUVAGE, LONDON, E.C.
15.386

Illustrated, Fine-Art, and other Volumes.

Art, The Magazine of. Yearly Vol. With 500 choice Engravings. 16s.
After London; or, Wild England. By Richard Jefferies. 3s. 6d.
Along Alaska's Great River. By F. Schwatka. Illustrated. 12s. 6d.
Appreciation of Gold. 6d.
Artist, Education of the. By E. Chesneau. Translated by Clara Bell. 5s.
Behind Time. By George Parsons Lathrop. Illustrated. 2s. 6d.
Bimetallism, The Theory of. By D. Barbour. 6s.
Bismarck, Prince. By Charles Lowe, M.A. Two Vols. 24s.
Bright, John, Life and Times of. By W. Robertson. 7s. 6d.
British Ballads. With 275 Original Illustrations. Two Vols. 7s. 6d. each.
British Battles on Land and Sea. By James Grant. With about 600 Illustrations. Three Vols., 4to, £1 7s.; Library Edition, £1 10s.
British Battles, Recent. Illustrated. 4to, 9s.; Library Edition, 10s.
Browning, An Introduction to the Study of. By A. Symons. 2s. 6d.
British Empire, The. By Sir George Campbell, M.P. 3s.
Butterflies and Moths, European. By W. F. Kirby. With 61 Coloured Plates. Demy 4to, 35s.
Canaries and Cage-Birds, The Illustrated Book of. By W. A. Blakston, W. Swaysland, and A. F. Wiener. With 56 Fac-simile Coloured Plates, 35s. Half-morocco, £2 5s.
Cannibals and Convicts. By Julian Thomas ("The Vagabond"). 10s. 6d.
Cassell's Family Magazine. Yearly Vol. Illustrated. 9s.
Cathedral Churches of England and Wales. Illustrated. 21s.
Celebrities of the Century: being a Dictionary of Men and Women of the Nineteenth Century. 21s.; Roxburgh, 25s.
Chess Problem, The. A Text-Book, with Illustrations. 7s. 6d.
Children of the Cold, The. By Lieut. Schwatka. 2s. 6d.
Choice Poems by H. W. Longfellow. Illustrated from Paintings by his Son, Ernest W. Longfellow. Small 4to, cloth, 6s.
Choice Dishes at Small Cost. By A. G. Payne. 1s.
Christmas in the Olden Time. By Sir Walter Scott, with charming Original Illustrations. 7s. 6d.
Cities of the World: their Origin, Progress, and Present Aspect. Three Vols. Illustrated. 7s. 6d. each.
Civil Service, Guide to Employment in the. 3s. 6d.
Civil Service.—Guide to Female Employment in Government Offices. 1s.
Clinical Manuals for Practitioners and Students of Medicine. A List of Volumes forwarded post free on application to the Publishers.
Clothing, The Influence of, on Health. By F. Treves, F.R.C.S. 2s.
Colonies and India, Our, How we Got Them, and Why we Keep Them. By Prof. C. Ransome. 1s.
Columbus, Christopher, The Life and Voyages of. By Washington Irving. Three Vols. 7s. 6d.
Cookery, Cassell's Dictionary of. Containing about Nine Thousand Recipes. 7s. 6d.; Roxburgh, 10s. 6d.
Co-operators, Working Men: What they have Done, and What they are Doing. By A. H. Dyke-Acland, M.P., and B. Jones. 1s.
Cookery, A Year's. By Phyllis Browne. 3s. 6d.
Cook Book, Catherine Owen's New. 4s.
Countries of the World, The. By Robert Brown, M.A., Ph.D., &c. Complete in Six Vols., with about 750 Illustrations. 4to, 7s. 6d. each.
Cromwell, Oliver: The Man and his Mission. By J. Allanson Picton, M.P. Cloth, 7s. 6d.; morocco, cloth sides, 9s.
Cyclopædia, Cassell's Concise. With 12,000 subjects, brought down to the latest date. With about 600 Illustrations, 15s.; Roxburgh, 18s.

Dairy Farming. By Prof. J. P. SHELDON. With 25 Fac-simile Coloured Plates, and numerous Wood Engravings. Cloth, 31s. 6d.; half-morocco, 42s.

Decisive Events in History. By THOMAS ARCHER. With Sixteen Illustrations. Boards, 3s. 6d.; cloth, 5s.

Decorative Design. By CHRISTOPHER DRESSER, Ph.D. Illustrated. 5s.

Deserted Village Series, The. Consisting of *Editions de luxe* of the most favourite poems of Standard Authors. Illustrated. 2s. 6d. each.

| SONGS FROM SHAKESPEARE. | GOLDSMITH'S DESERTED VILLAGE. |
| MILTON'S L'ALLEGRO AND IL PENSEROSO. | WORDSWORTH'S ODE ON IMMORTALITY, AND LINES ON TINTERN ABBEY. |

Dickens, Character Sketches from. SECOND and THIRD SERIES. With Six Original Drawings in each by F. BARNARD. In Portfolio, 21s. each.

Diary of Two Parliaments. By W. H. LUCY. Vol. I.: The Disraeli Parliament. Vol. II.: The Gladstone Parliament. 12s. each.

Dog, The. By IDSTONE. Illustrated. 2s. 6d.

Dog, Illustrated Book of the. By VERO SHAW, B.A. With 28 Coloured Plates. Cloth bevelled, 35s.; half-morocco, 45s.

Domestic Dictionary, The. Cloth, 7s. 6d.

Doré's Adventures of Munchausen. Illustrated by GUSTAVE DORÉ. 5s.

Doré's Dante's Inferno. Illustrated by GUSTAVE DORÉ. 21s.

Doré's Fairy Tales Told Again. With Engravings by DORÉ. 5s.

Doré Gallery, The. With 250 Illustrations by DORÉ. 4to, 42s.

Doré's Milton's Paradise Lost. Illustrated by DORÉ. 4to, 21s.

Edinburgh, Old and New. Three Vols. With 600 Illustrations. 9s. each.

Egypt: Descriptive, Historical, and Picturesque. By Prof. G. EBERS. Translated by CLARA BELL, with Notes by SAMUEL BIRCH, LL.D., &c. Two Vols. With 800 Original Engravings. Vol. I., £2 5s.; Vol. II., £2 12s. 6d. Complete in box, £4 17s. 6d.

Electricity in the Service of Man. With nearly 850 Illustrations. 21s.

Electricity, Practical. By Prof. W. E. AYRTON. 7s. 6d.

Electricity, Age of, from Amber Soul to Telephone. By PARK BENJAMIN, Ph.D. 7s. 6d.

Electrician's Pocket-Book, The. By GORDON WIGAN, M.A. 5s.

Encyclopædic Dictionary, The. A New and Original Work of Reference to all the Words in the English Language. Eleven Divisional Vols. now ready, 10s. 6d. each; or the Double Divisional Vols., half-morocco, 21s. each.

Energy in Nature. By WM. LANT CARPENTER, B.A., B.Sc. 80 Illustrations. 3s. 6d.

England, Cassell's Illustrated History of. With 2,000 Illustrations. Ten Vols., 4to, 9s. each.

English History, The Dictionary of. Cloth, 21s.; Roxburgh, 25s.

English Literature, Library of. By Prof. HENRY MORLEY. Five Vols., 7s. 6d. each.

VOL. I.—SHORTER ENGLISH POEMS.
VOL. II.—ILLUSTRATIONS OF ENGLISH RELIGION.
VOL. III.—ENGLISH PLAYS.
VOL IV.—SHORTER WORKS IN ENGLISH PROSE.
VOL. V.—SKETCHES OF LONGER WORKS IN ENGLISH VERSE AND PROSE.

Five Volumes handsomely bound in half-morocco, £5 5s.

English Literature, The Story of. By ANNA BUCKLAND. 3s. 6d.

English Literature, Morley's First Sketch of. *Revised Edition,* 7s. 6d.

English Literature, Dictionary of. By W. DAVENPORT ADAMS. *Cheap Edition*, 7s. 6d. ; Roxburgh, 10s. 6d.

English Poetesses. By ERIC S. ROBERTSON, M.A. 5s.

English Writers. By Prof. HENRY MORLEY. Vol. I. Crown 8vo, cloth, 5s.

Etching. By S. K. KOEHLER. With 30 Full-Page Plates by Old and Modern Etchers. £4 4s.

Etiquette of Good Society. 1s. ; cloth, 1s. 6d.

Exceptional Distress. 6d.

Eye, Ear, and Throat, The Management of the. 3s. 6d.

False Hopes. By Prof. GOLDWIN SMITH, M.A., LL.D., D.C.L. 6d.

Family Physician, The. By Eminent PHYSICIANS and SURGEONS. Cloth, 21s. ; half-morocco, 25s.

Fenn, G. Manville, Works by. Cloth boards, 2s. each.

SWEET MACE.
DUTCH THE DIVER.
MY PATIENTS. Being the Notes of a Navy Surgeon.

THE VICAR'S PEOPLE.
CODWEB'S FATHER.
THE PARSON O' DUMFORD.
POVERTY CORNER.

Ferns, European. By JAMES BRITTEN, F.L.S. With 30 Fac-simile Coloured Plates by D. BLAIR, F.L.S. 21s.

Field Naturalist's Handbook, The. By the Rev. J. G. WOOD and THEODORE WOOD. 5s.

Figuier's Popular Scientific Works. With Several Hundred Illustrations in each. 3s. 6d. each.

THE HUMAN RACE.
WORLD BEFORE THE DELUGE.
REPTILES AND BIRDS.

THE OCEAN WORLD.
THE VEGETABLE WORLD.
THE INSECT WORLD.

MAMMALIA.

Fine-Art Library, The. Edited by JOHN SPARKES, Principal of the South Kensington Art Schools. Each Book contains about 100 Illustrations. 5s. each.

ENGRAVING. By Le Vicomte Henri Delaborde. Translated by R. A. M. Stevenson.

TAPESTRY. By Eugène Müntz. Translated by Miss L. J. Davis.

THE ENGLISH SCHOOL OF PAINTING. By E. Chesneau. Translated by L. N. Etherington. With an Introduction by Prof. Ruskin.

THE FLEMISH SCHOOL OF PAINTING. By A. J. Wauters. Translated by Mrs. Henry Rossel.

THE EDUCATION OF THE ARTIST. By Ernest Chesneau. Translated by Clara Bell. (Not illustrated.)

GREEK ARCHÆOLOGY. By Maxime Collignon. Translated by Dr. J. H. Wright.

ARTISTIC ANATOMY. By Prof. Duval. Translated by F. E. Fenton.

THE DUTCH SCHOOL OF PAINTING. By Henry Havard. Translated by G. Powell.

Fisheries of the World, The. Illustrated. 4to. 9s.

Five Pound Note, The, and other Stories. By G. S. JEALOUS. 1s.

Flowers, and How to Paint Them. By MAUD NAFTEL. With Coloured Plates. 5s.

Forging of the Anchor, The. A Poem. By Sir SAMUEL FERGUSON. LL.D. With 20 Original Illustrations. Gilt edges, 5s.

Fossil Reptiles, A History of British. By Sir RICHARD OWEN, K.C.B., F.R.S., &c. With 268 Plates. In Four Vols., £12 12s.

Four Years of Irish History (1845-49). By Sir GAVAN DUFFY, K.C.M.G. 21s.

Franco-German War, Cassell's History of the. Two Vols. With 500 Illustrations. 9s. each.

Fresh-water Fishes of Europe, The. By Prof. H. G. SEELEY, F.R.S. Cloth, 21s.

From Gold to Grey. Being Poems and Pictures of Life and Nature. By MARY D. BRINE. Illustrated. 7s. 6d.

Garden Flowers, Familiar. By SHIRLEY HIBBERD. With Coloured Plates by F. E. HULME, F.L.S. Complete in Five Series. 12s. 6d. each.

Gardening, Cassell's Popular. Illustrated. 4 vols., 5s. each.

Geometrical Drawing for Army Candidates. By H. T. LILLEY, M.A. 2s.

Geometry, Practical Solid. By MAJOR ROSS. 2s.

Gladstone, Life of W. E. By G. BARNETT SMITH. With Portrait, 3s. 6d. *Jubilee Edition*, 1s.

Gleanings from Popular Authors. Two Vols. With Original Illustrations. 4to, 9s. each. Two Vols. in One, 15s.

Great Industries of Great Britain. Three Vols. With about 400 Illustrations. 4to, cloth, 7s. 6d. each.

Great Painters of Christendom, The, from Cimabue to Wilkie. By JOHN FORBES-ROBERTSON. Illustrated throughout. 12s. 6d.

Great Northern Railway, The Official Illustrated Guide to the. 1s.; or in cloth, 2s.

Great Western Railway, The Official Illustrated Guide to the. *New and Revised Edition.* With Illustrations, 1s.; cloth, 2s.

Gulliver's Travels. With 88 Engravings by MORTEN. *Cheap Edition.* Cloth, 3s. 6d.; cloth gilt, 5s.

Gun and its Development, The. By W. W. GREENER. With 500 Illustrations. 10s. 6d.

Health, The Book of. By Eminent Physicians and Surgeons. Cloth, 21s.; half-morocco, 25s.

Health, The Influence of Clothing on. By F. TREVES, F.R.G.S. 2s.

Health at School. By CLEMENT DUKES, M.D., B.S. 7s. 6d.

Heavens, The Story of the. By Sir ROBERT STAWELL BALL, F.R.S., F.R.A.S. With Coloured Plates and Wood Engravings. 31s. 6d.

Heroes of Britain in Peace and War. In Two Vols., with 300 Original Illustrations. 5s. each; or One Vol., library binding, 10s. 6d.

Horse Keeper, The Practical. By GEORGE FLEMING, L.L.D., F.R.C.V.S. Illustrated. 7s. 6d.

Horse, The Book of the. By SAMUEL SIDNEY With 28 *fac-simile* Coloured Plates. *Enlarged Edition.* Demy 4to, 35s.; half-morocco, 45s.

Horses, The Simple Ailments of. By W. F. Illustrated. 5s.

Household Guide, Cassell's. With Illustrations and Coloured Plates. *New and Cheap Edition*, in Four Vols., 20s.

How Women may Earn a Living. By MERCY GROGAN. 1s.

Imperial White Books. In Quarterly Vols. 10s. 6d. per annum, post free; separately, 3s. 6d. each.

India, The Coming Struggle for. By Prof. VAMBÉRY. 5s.

India, Cassell's History of. By JAMES GRANT. With about 400 Illustrations. Library binding. One Vol. 15s.

India: the Land and the People. By Sir J. CAIRD, K.C.B. 10s. 6d.

Indoor Amusements, Card Games, and Fireside Fun, Cassell's Book of. Illustrated. 3s. 6d.

Invisible Life, Vignettes from. By JOHN BADCOCK, F.R.M.S. Illustrated. 3s. 6d.

Irish Parliament, The; What it Was and What it Did. By J. G. SWIFT MACNEILL, M.A., M.P. 1s.

Italy. By J. W. PROBYN. 7s. 6d.

John Parmelee's Curse. By JULIAN HAWTHORNE. 2s. 6d.

Kennel Guide, The Practical. By Dr. GORDON STABLES. Illustrated. 2s. 6d.

Khiva, A Ride to. By the late Col. FRED. BURNABY. 1s. 6d.

Kidnapped. By R. L. STEVENSON. 5s.

Ladies' Physician, The. A Guide for Women in the Treatment of their Ailments. By a Physician. 6s.

Land Question, The. By Prof. J. ELLIOT, M.R.A.C. 10s. 6d.

Landscape Painting in Oils, A Course of Lessons in. By A. F. GRACE. With Nine Reproductions in Colour. *Cheap Edition*, 25s.

Law, About Going to. By A. J. WILLIAMS, M.P. 2s. 6d.

Letts's Diaries and other Time-saving Publications are now published exclusively by CASSELL & COMPANY. (*A list sent post free on application.*)

Liberal, Why I am a. By ANDREW REID. 2s. 6d. *People's Edition.* 1s.

Local Dual Standards. By JOHN HENRY NORMAN. 1s.

London and South Western Railway, The Official Illustrated Guide to the. 1s.; cloth, 2s.

London and North Western Railway, The Official Illustrated Guide to the. 1s.; cloth, 2s.

London, Greater. By EDWARD WALFORD. Two Vols. With about 400 Illustrations. 9s. each.

London, Old and New. Six Vols., each containing about 200 Illustrations and Maps. Cloth, 9s. each.

London's Roll of Fame. With Portraits and Illustrations. 12s. 6d.

Longfellow's Poetical Works. Illustrated throughout, £3 3s.; *Popular Edition*, 16s.

Love's Extremes, At. By MAURICE THOMPSON. 5s.

Martin Luther: His Life and Times. By PETER BAYNE, LL.D. Two Vols., demy 8vo, 1,040 pages. Cloth, 24s.

Mechanics, The Practical Dictionary of. Containing 15,000 Drawings. Four Vols. 21s. each.

Medicine, Manuals for Students of. (*A List forwarded post free.*)

Medical Sciences, International Journal of the. Quarterly Numbers. Each 6s.

Midland Railway, Official Illustrated Guide to the. *New and Revised Edition.* 1s.; cloth, 2s.

Modern Artists, Some. With highly-finished Engravings. 12s. 6d.

Modern Europe, A History of. By C. A. FYFFE, M.A. Vol. I., from 1792 to 1814. 12s. Vol. II., from 1814 to 1848. 12s.

Music, Illustrated History of. By EMIL NAUMANN. Edited by the Rev. Sir F. A. GORE OUSELEY, Bart. Illustrated. Two Vols. 31s. 6d.

National Library, Cassell's. In Weekly Volumes, each containing about 192 pages. Paper covers, 3d.; cloth, 6d. (*A List sent post free on application.*)

Natural History, Cassell's Concise. By E. PERCEVAL WRIGHT, M.A., M.D., F.L.S. With several Hundred Illustrations. 7s. 6d.

Natural History, Cassell's New. Edited by Prof. P. MARTIN DUNCAN, M.B., F.R.S., F.G.S. With Contributions by Eminent Scientific Writers. Complete in Six Vols. With about 2,000 high-class Illustrations. Extra crown 4to, cloth, 9s. each.

Nature, Short Studies from. Illustrated. 5s.

Nimrod in the North; or, Hunting and Fishing Adventures in the Arctic Regions. By F. SCHWATKA. Illustrated. 7s. 6d.

Nursing for the Home and for the Hospital, A Handbook of. By CATHERINE J. WOOD. *Cheap Edition.* 1s. 6d.; cloth, 2s.

Oil Painting, A Manual of. By the Hon. JOHN COLLIER. 2s. 6d.

Our Homes, and How to Make them Healthy. By Eminent Authorities. Illustrated. 15s.; half-morocco, 21s.

Our Own Country. Six Vols. With 1,200 Illustrations. 7s. 6d. each.

Painting, Practical Guides to. With Coloured Plates and full instructions:—Animal Painting, 5s.—China Painting, 5s.—Figure Painting, 7s. 6d.—Flower Painting, 2 Books, 5s. each.—Tree Painting, 5s.—Water-Colour Painting, 5s.—Neutral Tint, 5s.—Sepia, in 2 Vols, 3s. each.—Flowers, and How to Paint Them, 5s.

Paris, Cassell's Illustrated Guide to. 1s. ; cloth, 2s.

Parliaments, A Diary of Two. By H. W. LUCY. The Disraeli Parliament, 1874—1880. 12s. The Gladstone Parliament, 1881—1886. 12s.

Paxton's Flower Garden. By Sir JOSEPH PAXTON and Prof. LINDLEY. Three Vols. With 100 Coloured Plates. £1 1s. each.

Peoples of the World, The. In Six Vols. By Dr. ROBERT BROWN. Illustrated. 7s. 6d. each.

Phantom City, The. By W. WESTALL. 5s.

Photography for Amateurs. By T. C. HEPWORTH. Illustrated. 1s. ; or cloth, 1s. 6d.

Phrase and Fable, Dictionary of. By the Rev. Dr. BREWER. *Cheap Edition, Enlarged*, cloth, 3s. 6d. ; or with leather back, 4s. 6d.

Picturesque America. Complete in Four Vols., with 48 Exquisite Steel Plates and about 800 Original Wood Engravings. £2 2s. each.

Picturesque Canada. With 600 Original Illustrations. Two Vols. £3 3s. each.

Picturesque Europe. Complete in Five Vols. Each containing 13 Exquisite Steel Plates, from Original Drawings, and nearly 200 Original Illustrations. £10 10s. The POPULAR EDITION is published in Five Vols., 18s. each.

Pigeon Keeper, The Practical. By LEWIS WRIGHT. Illustrated. 3s. 6d.

Pigeons, The Book of. By ROBERT FULTON. Edited and Arranged by L. WRIGHT. With 50 Coloured Plates, 31s. 6d. ; half-morocco, £2 2s.

Poems and Pictures. With numerous Illustrations. 5s.

Poets, Cassell's Miniature Library of the :—

BURNS. Two Vols. 2s. 6d.	MILTON. Two Vols. 2s. 6d.
BYRON. Two Vols. 2s. 6d.	SCOTT. Two Vols. 2s. 6d. [2s. 6d.
HOOD. Two Vols. 2s. 6d.	SHERIDAN and GOLDSMITH. 2 Vols.
LONGFELLOW. Two Vols. 2s. 6d.	WORDSWORTH. Two Vols. 2s. 6d.

SHAKESPEARE. Twelve Vols., in Case, 15s.

• *The above are also publishing in cloth. 1s. each Vol.*

Police Code, and Manual of the Criminal Law. By C. E. HOWARD VINCENT, M.P. 2s.

Popular Library, Cassell's. Cloth, 1s. each.

The Russian Empire.	The Story of the English Jacobins.
The Religious Revolution in the 16th Century.	Domestic Folk Lore.
English Journalism.	The Rev. Rowland Hill : Preacher and Wit.
Our Colonial Empire.	Boswell and Johnson : their Companions and Contemporaries.
John Wesley.	The Scottish Covenanters.
The Young Man in the Battle of Life.	History of the Free-Trade Movement in England.

Poultry Keeper, The Practical. By L. WRIGHT. With Coloured Plates and Illustrations. 3s. 6d.

Poultry, The Illustrated Book of. By L. WRIGHT. With Fifty Coloured Plates. Cloth, 31s. 6d. ; half-morocco, £2 2s.

Poultry, The Book of. By LEWIS WRIGHT. *Popular Edition.* 10s. 6d.

Quiver Yearly Volume, The. With about 300 Original Contributions by Eminent Divines and Popular Authors, and upwards of 250 high-class Illustrations. 7s. 6d.

Rabbit-Keeper, The Practical. By CUNICULUS. Illustrated. 3s. 6d.

Red Library, Cassell's. Stiff covers, 1s. each; cloth, 2s. each; or half-calf, marbled edges, 5s. each.

Deerslayer.	Yellowplush Papers.
Eugene Aram.	Handy Andy. [Book.
Jack Hinton, the Guardsman.	Washington Irving's Sketch-
Rome and the Early Christians.	Last Days of Pa'myra.
The Trials of Margaret Lyndsay.	Tales of the Borders.
Old Mortality.	American Humour.
The Hour and the Man.	Sketches by Boz. [Essays.
Scarlet Letter.	Macaulay's Lays and Selected
Poe's Works.	Harry Lorrequer.
Pride and Prejudice.	Old Curiosity Shop.
Last of the Mohicans.	Rienzi.
Heart of Midlothian.	The Talisman.
Last Days of Pompeii.	Pickwick (2 Vols.)

Representative Poems of Living Poets American and English. Selected by the Poets themselves. 15s.

Royal River, The : The Thames from Source to Sea. With Descriptive Text and a Series of beautiful Engravings. £2 2s.

Russia. By Sir DONALD MACKENZIE WALLACE, M.A 5s.

Russo-Turkish War, Cassell's History of. With about 500 Illustrations. Two Vols., 9s. each.

Sandwith, Humphry. A Memoir by T. H. WARD. 7s. 6d.

Saturday Journal, Cassell's. Yearly Volume. 6s.

Science for All. Edited by Dr. ROBERT BROWN, M.A., F.L.S., &c. With 1,500 Illustrations. Five Vols. 9s. each.

Sea, The: Its Stirring Story of Adventure, Peril, and Heroism. By F. WHYMPER. With 400 Illustrations. Four Vols., 7s. 6d. each.

Sent Back by the Angels. And other Ballads. By FREDERICK LANG-BRIDGE, M.A. Cloth, 4s. 6d.

Shaftesbury, The Seventh Earl of, K.G., The Life and Work of. By EDWIN HODDER. With Portraits. Three Vols., 36s.

Shakspere, The Leopold. With 400 Illustrations. Cloth, 6s. ; cloth gilt, 7s. 6d. ; half-morocco, 10s. 6d.

Shakspere, The Royal. With Steel Plates and Wood Engravings. Three Vols. 15s. each.

Shakespeare, Cassell's Quarto Edition. Edited by CHARLES and MARY COWDEN CLARKE, and containing about 600 Illustrations by H. C. SELOUS. Complete in Three Vols., cloth gilt, £3 3s.

Shakespeare's Romeo and Juliet. *Edition de Luxe.* Illustrated with Twelve Superb Photogravures from Original Drawings by F. DICKSEE, A.R.A. £5 5s.

Shakespearean Scenes and Characters. With 30 Steel Plates and 10 Wood Engravings. The Text written by AUSTIN BRERETON. 21s.

Sketching from Nature in Water Colours. By AARON PENLEY. With Illustrations in Chromo-Lithography. 15s.

Skin and Hair, The Management of the. By MALCOLM MORRIS, F.R.C.S. 2s.

Smith, The Adventures and Discourses of Captain John. By JOHN ASHTON. Illustrated. 5s.

Sports and Pastimes, Cassell's Book of. With more than 800 Illustrations and Coloured Frontispiece. 768 pages. 9s. (Can be had separately thus: Outdoor Sports, 7s. 6d. ; Indoor Amusements, 3s. 6d.)

Steam Engine, The Theory and Action of the : for Practical Men. By W. H. NORTHCOTT, C.E. 3s. 6d.

Stock Exchange Year-Book, The. By THOMAS SKINNER. 10s. 6d.

Stones of London, The. By E. F. FLOWER. 6d.

" Stories from Cassell's." A Series of Seven Books. 6d. each ; cloth lettered, 9d. each.

Sunlight and Shade. With numerous Exquisite Engravings. 7s. 6d.

Surgery, Memorials of the Craft of, in England. With an Introduction by Sir JAMES PAGET. 21s.

Telegraph Guide, The. Illustrated. 1s.

Thackeray, Character Sketches from. Six New and Original Draw-ings by FREDERICK BARNARD, reproduced in Photogravure. 21s.

Trajan. An American Novel. By H. F. KEENAN. 7s. 6d.

Transformations of Insects, The. By Prof. P. MARTIN DUNCAN, M.B., F.R.S. With 240 Illustrations. 6s.

Treasure Island. By R. L. STEVENSON. Illustrated. 5s.

Treatment, The Year-Book of. A Critical Review for Practitioners of Medicine and Surgery. 5s.

Trees, Familiar. First Series. By G. S. BOULGER, F.L.S., F.G.S. With 40 full page Coloured Plates, from Original Paintings by W. H. J. BOOT. 12s. 6d.

Twenty Photogravures of Pictures in the Salon of 1885, by the leading French Artists.

" Unicode ": the Universal Telegraphic Phrase Book. 2s. 6d. each.

United States, Cassell's History of the. By EDMUND OLLIER. With 600 Illustrations. Three Vols. 9s. each.

Universal History, Cassell's Illustrated. Four Vols. 9s. each.

Vicar of Wakefield and other Works by OLIVER GOLDSMITH. Illustrated. 3s. 6d.; cloth, gilt edges, 5s.

Wealth-Creation. By AUGUSTUS MONGREDIEN. 5s.

Westall, W., Novels by. *Popular Editions.* Cloth, 2s. each.

RALPH NORBRECK'S TRUST.

| THE OLD FACTORY. | RED RYVINGTON. |

What Girls Can Do. By PHYLLIS BROWNE. 2s. 6d.

Wild Animals and Birds: their Haunts and Habits. By Dr. ANDREW WILSON. Illustrated. 7s. 6d.

Wild Birds, Familiar. First and Second Series. By W. SWAYSLAND. With 40 Coloured Plates in each. 12s. 6d. each.

Wild Flowers, Familiar. By F. E. HULME, F.L.S., F.S.A. Five Series. With 40 Coloured Plates in each. 12s. 6d. each.

Winter in India, A. By the Rt. Hon. W. E. BAXTER, M.P. 5s.

Wise Woman, The. By GEORGE MACDONALD. 2s. 6d.

Wood Magic: A Fable. By RICHARD JEFFERIES. 6s.

World of the Sea. Translated from the French of MOQUIN TANDON, by the Very Rev. H. MARTYN HART, M.A. Illustrated. Cloth. 6s.

World of Wit and Humour, The. With 400 Illustrations. Cloth, 7s. 6d.; cloth gilt, gilt edges, 10s. 6d.

World of Wonders. Two Vols. With 400 Illustrations. 7s. 6d. each.

Yule Tide. Cassell's Christmas Annual, 1s.

MAGAZINES.

The Quiver, for Sunday Reading. Monthly, 6d.

Cassell's Family Magazine. Monthly, 7d.

"Little Folks" Magazine. Monthly, 6d.

The Magazine of Art. Monthly, 1s.

The Lady's World. Monthly, 1s.

Cassell's Saturday Journal. Weekly, 1d.; Monthly, 6d.

Bibles and Religious Works.

Bible, The Crown Illustrated. With about 1,000 Original Illustrations. With References, &c. 1,248 pages, crown 4to, cloth, 7s. 6d.

Bible, Cassell's Illustrated Family. With 900 Illustrations. Leather, gilt edges, £2 10s.

Bible Dictionary, Cassell's. With nearly 600 Illustrations. 7s. 6d.

Bible Educator, The. Edited by the Very Rev. Dean PLUMPTRE, D.D., Wells. With Illustrations, Maps, &c. Four Vols., cloth, 6s. each.

Bible Work at Home and Abroad. Volume. Illustrated. 3s.

Bunyan's Pilgrim's Progress (Cassell's Illustrated). Demy 4to. Illustrated throughout. 7s. 6d.

Bunyan's Pilgrim's Progress. With Illustrations. Cloth, 3s. 6d.

Child's Life of Christ, The. With 200 Illustrations. 21s.

Child's Bible, The. With 200 Illustrations. 143rd *Thousand*. 7s. 6d.

Church at Home, The. A Series of Short Sermons. By the Rt. Rev. ROWLEY HILL, D.D., Bishop of Sodor and Man. 5s.

Day-Dawn in Dark Places; or, Wanderings and Work in Bechwanaland. By the Rev. JOHN MACKENZIE. Illustrated. 3s. 6d.

Dictionary of Religion, The. An Encyclopædia of Christian and other Religious Doctrines, Denominations, Sects, Heresies, Ecclesiastical Terms, History, Biography, &c. &c. By the Rev. WILLIAM BENHAM, B.D. Cloth, 21s.; Roxburgh, 25s.

Doré Bible. With 230 Illustrations by GUSTAVE DORÉ. Cloth, £2 10s.

Early Days of Christianity, The. By the Ven. Archdeacon FARRAR, D.D., F.R.S.
> LIBRARY EDITION. Two Vols., 24s.; morocco, £2 2s.
> POPULAR EDITION. Complete in One Volume, cloth, 6s.; cloth, gilt edges, 7s. 6d.; Persian morocco, 10s. 6d.; tree-calf, 15s.

Family Prayer-Book, The. Edited by Rev. Canon GARBETT. M.A., and Rev. S. MARTIN. Extra crown 4to, cloth, 5s.; morocco, 18s.

Geikie, Cunningham, D.D., Works by:—
> HOURS WITH THE BIBLE. Six Vols., 6s. each.
> ENTERING ON LIFE. 3s. 6d.
> THE PRECIOUS PROMISES. 2s. 6d.
> THE ENGLISH REFORMATION. 5s.
> OLD TESTAMENT CHARACTERS. 6s.
> THE LIFE AND WORDS OF CHRIST. Two Vols., cloth, 30s. *Students' Edition.* Two Vols., 16s.

Glories of the Man of Sorrows, The. By Rev. H. G. BONAVIA HUNT, F.R.S., Ed.: Evening preacher at St. James's, Piccadilly. 2s. 6d.

Gospel of Grace, The. By a LINDESIE. Cloth, 3s. 6d.

"Heart Chords." A Series of Works by Eminent Divines. Bound in cloth, red edges, One Shilling each.

My Father.	My Aspirations.	My Hereafter.
My Bible.	My Emotional Life.	My Walk with God.
My Work for God.	My Body.	My Aids to the Divine Life.
	My Soul.	
My Object in Life.	My Growth in Divine Life.	My Sources of Strength.

Helps to Belief. A Series of Helpful Manuals on the Religious Difficulties of the Day. Edited by the Rev. TEIGNMOUTH SHORE, M.A., Chaplain-in-Ordinary to the Queen. Cloth, 1s. each.

CREATION. By the Lord Bishop of Carlisle.	MIRACLES. By the Rev. Brownlow Maitland, M.A.
THE DIVINITY OF OUR LORD. By the Lord Bishop of Derry.	PRAYER. By the Rev. T. Teignmouth Shore, M.A.
	THE RESURRECTION. By the Lord Archbishop of York.
THE MORALITY OF THE OLD TESTAMENT. By the Rev. Newman Smyth, D.D.	THE ATONEMENT. By the Lord Bishop of Peterborough.

Lay Texts for the Young. In English and French. By Mrs. RICHARD STRACHEY. 2s. 6d.

Life of Christ, The. By the Ven. Archdeacon FARRAR, D.D., F.R.S.
ILLUSTRATED EDITION, with about 300 Original Illustrations. Extra crown 4to, cloth, gilt edges, 21s. ; morocco antique, 42s.
LIBRARY EDITION. Two Vols. Cloth, 24s. ; morocco, 42s.
BIJOU EDITION. Five Volumes, in box, 10s. 6d. the set.
POPULAR EDITION, in One Vol. 8vo, cloth, 6s. ; cloth, gilt edges, 7s. 6d. ; Persian morocco, gilt edges, 10s. 6d. ; tree-calf, 15s.

Marriage Ring, The. By WILLIAM LANDELS, D.D. Bound in white leatherette, gilt edges, in box, 6s. ; morocco, 8s. 6d.

Moses and Geology ; or, The Harmony of the Bible with Science. By the Rev. SAMUEL KINNS, Ph.D., F.R.A.S. Illustrated. *Cheap Edition*, 6s.

Music of the Bible, The. By J. STAINER, M.A., Mus. Doc. 2s. 6d.

New Testament Commentary for English Readers, The. Edited by the Rt. Rev. C. J. ELLICOTT, D.D., Lord Bishop of Gloucester and Bristol. In Three Volumes, 21s. each.
Vol. I.—The Four Gospels.
Vol. II.—The Acts, Romans, Corinthians, Galatians.
Vol. III.—The remaining Books of the New Testament.

Old Testament Commentary for English Readers, The. Edited by the Right Rev. C. J. ELLICOTT, D.D., Lord Bishop of Gloucester and Bristol. Complete in 5 Vols., 21s. each.
Vol. I.—Genesis to Numbers.
Vol. II.—Deuteronomy to Samuel II.
Vol. III.—Kings I. to Esther.
Vol. IV.—Job to Isaiah.
Vol. V.—Jeremiah to Malachi.

Patriarchs, The. By the late Rev. W. HANNA, D.D., and the Ven. Archdeacon NORRIS, B.D. 2s. 6d.

Protestantism, The History of. By the Rev. J. A. WYLIE, LL.D. Containing upwards of 600 Original Illustrations. Three Vols., 27s.

Quiver Yearly Volume, The. 250 high-class Illustrations. 7s. 6d.

Revised Version—Commentary on the Revised Version of the New Testament. By the Rev. W. G. HUMPHRY, B.D. 7s. 6d.

Sacred Poems, The Book of. Edited by the Rev. Canon BAYNES, M.A. With Illustrations. Cloth, gilt edges, 5s.

St. George for England ; and other Sermons preached to Children. By the Rev. T. TEIGNMOUTH SHORE, M.A. 5s.

St. Paul, The Life and Work of. By the Ven. Archdeacon FARRAR, D.D., F.R.S., Chaplain-in-Ordinary to the Queen.
LIBRARY EDITION. Two Vols., cloth, 24s. ; morocco, 42s.
ILLUSTRATED EDITION, complete in One Volume, with about 300 Illustrations, £1 1s. ; morocco, £2 2s.
POPULAR EDITION. One Volume, 8vo, cloth, 6s.; cloth, gilt edges, 7s. 6d. ; Persian morocco, 10s. 6d. ; tree-calf, 15s.

Secular Life, The Gospel of the. Sermons preached at Oxford. By the Hon. W. H. FREMANTLE, Canon of Canterbury. 5s.

Sermons Preached at Westminster Abbey. By ALFRED BARRY, D.D., D.C.L., Primate of Australia. 5s.

Shall We Know One Another ? By the Rt. Rev. J. C RYLE, D.D., Bishop of Liverpool. *New and Enlarged Edition.* Cloth limp, 1s.

Simon Peter: His Life, Times, and Friends. By E. HODDER. 5s.

Twilight of Life, The. Words of Counsel and Comfort for the Aged. By the Rev. JOHN ELLERTON, M.A. 1s. 6d.

Voice of Time, The. By JOHN STROUD. Cloth gilt, 1s.

Educational Works and Students' Manuals.

Alphabet, Cassell's Pictorial. 3s. 6d.

Algebra, The Elements of. By Prof. WALLACE, M.A. 1s.

Arithmetics, The Modern School. By GEORGE RICKS, B.Sc. Lond. With Test Cards. (*List on application.*)

Book-Keeping. By THEODORE JONES. For Schools, 2s. ; cloth, 3s. For the Million, 2s. ; cloth, 3s. Books for Jones's System. 2s.

Chemistry, The Public School. By J. H. ANDERSON, M.A. 2s. 6d.

Commentary, The New Testament. Edited by the Lord Bishop of GLOUCESTER and BRISTOL. Handy Volume Edition. St. Matthew, 3s. 6d. St. Mark, 3s. St. Luke, 3s. 6d. St. John, 3s. 6d. The Acts of the Apostles, 3s. 6d. Romans, 2s. 6d. Corinthians I. and II., 3s. Galatians, Ephesians, and Philippians, 3s. Colossians, Thessalonians, and Timothy, 3s. Titus, Philemon, Hebrews, and James, 3s. Peter, Jude, and John, 3s. The Revelation, 3s. An Introduction to the New Testament, 3s. 6d.

Commentary, Old Testament. Edited by Bishop ELLICOTT. Handy Volume Edition. Genesis, 3s. 6d. Exodus, 3s. Leviticus, 3s. Numbers, 2s. 6d. Deuteronomy, 2s. 6d.

Copy-Books, Cassell's Graduated. *Eighteen Books.* 2d. each.

Copy-Books, The Modern School. *Twelve Books.* 2d. each.

Drawing Books, Cassell's New Standard. 7 Books. 2d. each.

Drawing Books, Superior. 4 Books. Price 5s. each.

Drawing Copies, Cassell's Modern School Freehand. First Grade, 1s. ; Second Grade, 2s.

Drawing Copies, Cassell's New Standard. Seven Books. 2d. each.

Electricity, Practical. By Prof. W. E. AYRTON. 7s. 6d.

Energy and Motion: A Text-Book of Elementary Mechanics. By WILLIAM PAICE, M.A. Illustrated. 1s. 6d.

English Literature, First Sketch of. *New and Enlarged Edition.* By Prof. MORLEY. 7s. 6d.

Euclid, Cassell's. Edited by Prof. WALLACE, M.A. 1s.

Euclid, The First Four Books of. In paper, 6d. ; cloth, 9d.

French Reader, Cassell's Public School. By GUILLAUME S. CONRAD. 2s. 6d.

French, Cassell's Lessons in. *New and Revised Edition.* Parts I. and II., each 2s. 6d. ; complete, 4s. 6d. Key, 1s. 6d.

French-English and English-French Dictionary. *Entirely New and Enlarged Edition.* 1,150 pages, 8vo. cloth, 3s. 6d.

Galbraith and Haughton's Scientific Manuals. By the Rev. Prof. GALBRAITH, M.A., and the Rev. Prof. HAUGHTON, M.D., D.C.L. Arithmetic, 3s. 6d.—Plane Trigonometry, 2s. 6d.—Euclid, Books I., II., III., 2s. 6d.—Books IV., V., VI., 2s. 6d.—Mathematical Tables, 3s. 6d.—Mechanics, 3s. 6d.—Optics, 2s. 6d.—Hydrostatics, 3s. 6d.—Astronomy, 5s.—Steam Engine, 3s. 6d.—Algebra, Part I., cloth, 2s. 6d. ; Complete, 7s. 6d.—Tides and Tidal Currents, with Tidal Cards, 3s.

Geometry, Practical Solid. By Major Ross, R.E. 2s.

German-English and English-German Dictionary. *Entirely New and Revised Edition.* 3s. 6d.

German Reading, First Lessons in. By A. JAGST. Illustrated. 1s.

German of To-Day. By Dr. HEINEMANN. 1s. 6d.

Handbook of New Code of Regulations. By JOHN F. MOSS. 1s.

Historical Course for Schools, Cassell's. Illustrated throughout. I.—Stories from English History, 1s. II.—The Simple Outline of English History, 1s. 3d. III.—The Class History of England, 2s. 6d.

Latin-English Dictionary, Cassell's. By J. R. V. MARCHANT, M.A. 3s. 6d.

Latin-English and English-Latin Dictionary. By J. R. BEARD, D.D., and C. BEARD, B.A. Crown 8vo, 914 pp., 3s. 6d.

Little Folks' History of England. By ISA CRAIG-KNOX. With 30 Illustrations. 1s. 6d.

Making of the Home, The: A Book of Domestic Economy for School and Home Use. By Mrs. SAMUEL A. BARNETT. 1s. 6d.

Marlborough Books:—Arithmetic Examples, 3s. Arithmetic Rules, 1s. 6d. French Exercises, 3s. 6d. French Grammar, 2s. 6d. German Grammar, 3s. 6d.

Music, An Elementary Manual of. By HENRY LESLIE. 1s.

Natural Philosophy. By Prof. HAUGHTON, F.R.S. Illustrated. 3s. 6d.

Popular Educator, Cassell's. *New and Thoroughly Revised Edition.* Illustrated throughout. Complete in Six Vols., 5s. each.

Physical Science, Intermediate Text-Book of. By F. H. BOWMAN, D.Sc., F.R.A.S., F.L.S. Illustrated. 3s. 6d.

Readers, Cassell's Readable. Carefully graduated, extremely interesting, and illustrated throughout. (*List on application.*)

Readers, Cassell's Historical. Illustrated throughout, printed on superior paper, and strongly bound in cloth. (*List on application.*)

Readers for Infant Schools, Coloured. Three Books. Each containing 48 pages, including 8 pages in colours. 4d. each.

Reader, The Citizen. By H. O. ARNOLD-FORSTER, with Preface by the late Right Hon. W. E. FORSTER, M.P. 1s. 6d.

Readers, The Modern Geographical, illustrated throughout, and strongly bound in cloth. (*List on application.*)

Readers, The Modern School. Illustrated. (*List on application.*)

Reading and Spelling Book, Cassell's Illustrated. 1s.

Right Lines; or, Form and Colour. With Illustrations. 1s.

School Bank Manual. By AGNES LAMBERT. Price 6d.

School Manager's Manual. By F. C. MILLS, M.A. 1s.

Shakspere's Plays for School Use. 5 Books. Illustrated, 6d. each.

Shakspere Reading Book, The. By H. COURTHOPE BOWEN, M.A. Illustrated. 3s. 6d. Also issued in Three Books, 1s. each.

Spelling, A Complete Manual of. By J. D. MORELL, LL.D. 1s.

Technical Manuals, Cassell's. Illustrated throughout:—
Handrailing and Staircasing, 3s. 6d.—Bricklayers, Drawing for, 3s.—Building Construction, 2s.—Cabinet-Makers, Drawing for, 3s.—Carpenters and Joiners, Drawing for, 3s. 6d.—Gothic Stonework, 3s.—Linear Drawing and Practical Geometry, 2s.—Linear Drawing and Projection. The Two Vols. in One, 3s. 6d.—Machinists and Engineers, Drawing for, 4s. 6d.—Metal-Plate Workers, Drawing for, 3s.—Model Drawing, 3s.—Orthographical and Isometrical Projection, 2s.—Practical Perspective, 3s.—Stonemasons, Drawing for, 3s.—Applied Mechanics, by Sir R. S. Ball, LL.D., 2s.—Systematic Drawing and Shading, 2s.

Technical Educator, Cassell's. Four Vols. 6s. each. *New and Cheap Edition,* in Four Vols., 5s. each.

Technology, Manuals of. Edited by Prof. AYRTON, F.R.S., and RICHARD WORMELL, D.Sc., M.A. Illustrated throughout:—
The Dyeing of Textile Fabrics, by Prof. Hummel, 5s.—Watch and Clock Making, by D. Glasgow, 4s. 6d.—Steel and Iron, by W. H. Greenwood, F.C.S., Assoc. M.I.C.E., &c., 5s.—Spinning Woollen and Worsted, by W. S. Bright McLaren, 4s. 6d.—Design in Textile Fabrics, by T. R. Ashenhurst, 4s. 6d.—Practical Mechanics, by Prof. Perry, M.E., 3s. 6d.—Cutting Tools Worked by Hand and Machine, by Prof. Smith, 3s. 6d. *A Prospectus on application.*

Test Cards, Cassell's Combination. In sets, 1s. each.

CASSELL & COMPANY, LIMITED, *Ludgate Hill, London.*

Books for Young People.

Books for Young People. Illustrated. Cloth gilt, 5s. each.

Under Bayard's Banner. By Henry Frith.

The King's Command: A Story for Girls. By Maggie Symington.

For Fortune and Glory: a Story of the Soudan War. By Lewis Hough.

The Tales of the Sixty Mandarins. By P. V. Ramaswami Raju. With an Introduction by Prof. Henry Morley.

"Follow My Leader;" or, the Boys of Templeton. By Talbot Baines Reed.

The Romance of Invention. By James Burnley.

The Champion of Odin: or, Viking Life in the Days of Old. By J. Fred. Hodgetts.

Bound by a Spell: or, the Hunted Witch of the Forest. By the Hon. Mrs. Greene.

Books for Young People. Illustrated. Price 3s. 6d. each.

A World of Girls: The Story of a School. By L. T. Meade.

Lost among White Africans: A Boy's Adventures on the Upper Congo. By David Ker.

Freedom's Sword: A Story of the Days of Wallace and Bruce. By Annie S. Swan.

On Board the "Esmeralda:" or, Martin Leigh's Log. By John C. Hutcheson.

In Quest of Gold: or, Under the Whanga Falls. By Alfred St. Johnston.

For Queen and King: or, the Loyal 'Prentice. By Henry Frith.

Perils Afloat and Brigands Ashore. By Alfred Elwes.

The "Cross and Crown" Series. Consisting of Stories founded on incidents which occurred during Religious Persecutions of Past Days. With Illustrations in each Book, printed on a tint. 2s. 6d. each.

Strong to Suffer: A Story of the Jews. By E. Wynne.

Heroes of the Indian Empire; or, Stories of Valour and Victory. By Ernest Foster.

In Letters of Flame: A Story of the Waldenses. By C. L. Matéaux.

Through Trial to Triumph. By Madeline B. Hunt.

By Fire and Sword: A Story of the Huguenots. By Thomas Archer.

Adam Hepburn's Vow: A Tale of Kirk and Covenant. By Annie S. Swan.

No. XIII.; or, The Story of the Lost Vestal. A Tale of Early Christian Days. By Emma Marshall.

The "Log Cabin" Series. By EDWARD S. ELLIS. With Four Full-age Illustrations in each. Crown 8vo, cloth, 2s. 6d. each.

The Lost Trail. | Camp-Fire and Wigwam. | Footprints in the Forest.

The "Great River" Series (uniform with the "Log Cabin" Series). By EDWARD S. ELLIS. Illustrated. Crown 8vo, cloth, bevelled boards, 2s. 6d. each.

Down the Mississippi. | Lost in the Wilds.
Up the Tapajos; or, Adventures in Brazil.

The "Boy Pioneer" Series. By EDWARD S. ELLIS. With Four Full-page Illustrations in each Book. Crown 8vo, cloth, 2s. 6d. each.

Ned in the Woods. A Tale of Early Days in the West. | Ned on the River. A Tale of Indian River Warfare.
Ned in the Block House. A Story of Pioneer Life in Kentucky.

"Golden Mottoes" Series, The. Each Book containing 208 pages, with Four full-page Original Illustrations. Crown 8vo, cloth gilt, 2s. each.

"Nil Desperandum." By the Rev. F. Langbridge.

"Bear and Forbear." By Sarah Pitt.

"Foremost if I Can." By Helen Atteridge.

"Honour is my Guide." By Jeanie Hering (Mrs. Adams-Acton).

"Aim at the Sure End." By Emilie Searchfield.

"He Conquers who Endures." By the Author of "May Cunningham's Trial," &c.

Sunday School Reward Books. By Popular Authors. With Four Original Illustrations in each. Cloth gilt, 1s. 6d. each.

Rhoda's Reward; or, "If Wishes were Horses."
Jack Marston's Anchor.
Frank's Life-Battle; or, The Three Friends.

Rags and Rainbows: a Story of Thanksgiving.
Uncle William's Charges; or, The Broken Trust.
Pretty Pink's Purpose; or, The Little Street Merchants.

The New Children's Album. Fcap. 4to, 320 pages. Illustrated throughout. 3s. 6d.

The History Scrap Book. With nearly 1,000 Engravings. 5s.; cloth, 7s. 6d.

"Little Folks" Half-Yearly Volume. With 200 Illustrations and several Pictures in Colour. 3s. 6d.; or cloth gilt, 5s.

The Merry-go-Round. Original Poems for Children. Illustrated throughout. 5s.

Bo-Peep. A Book for the Little Ones. With Original Stories and Verses, Illustrated throughout. Boards, 2s. 6d.; cloth gilt, 3s. 6d.

The World's Lumber Room. By SELINA GAYE. Illustrated. 3s. 6d.

The "Proverbs" Series. Original Stories by Popular Authors, founded on and illustrating well-known Proverbs. With Four Illustrations in each Book, printed on a tint. 1s. 6d. each.

Fritters. By Sarah Pitt.
Trixy. By Maggie Symington.
The Two Hardcastles. By Madeline Bonavia Hunt.
Major Monk's Motto. By the Rev. F. Langbridge.

Tim Thomson's Trial. By George Weatherly.
Ursula's Stumbling-Block. By Julia Goddard.
Ruth's Life-Work. By the Rev. Joseph Johnson.

The World's Workers. A Series of New and Original Volumes. With Portraits printed on a tint as Frontispiece. 1s. each.

General Gordon. By the Rev. S. A. Swaine.
Charles Dickens. By his Eldest Daughter.
Sir Titus Salt and George Moore. By J. Burnley.
Florence Nightingale, Catherine Marsh, Frances Ridley Havergal, Mrs. Ranyard ("L.N.R."). By Lizzie Alldridge.
Dr. Guthrie, Father Mathew, Elihu Burritt, George Livesey. By the Rev. J. W. Kirton.
David Livingstone. By Robert Smiles.

Sir Henry Havelock and Colin Campbell, Lord Clyde. By E. C. Phillips.
Abraham Lincoln. By Ernest Foster.
George Müller and Andrew Reed. By E. R. Pitman.
Richard Cobden. By R. Gowing.
Benjamin Franklin. By E. M. Tomkinson.
Handel. By Eliza Clarke.
Turner the Artist. By the Rev. S. A. Swaine.
George and Robert Stephenson. By C. L. Matéaux.

The "Chimes" Series. Each containing 64 pages, with Illustrations on every page, and bound in Japanese morocco, 1s.

Bible Chimes.
Daily Chimes.

Holy Chimes.
Old World Chimes.

Sixpenny Story Books. All Illustrated, and containing Interesting Stories by well-known Writers.

Little Content.
The Smuggler's Cave.
Little Lizzie.
Little Bird.
The Boot on the Wrong Foot.
Luke Barnicott.
Little Pickles.
The Boat Club. By Oliver Optic.

Helpful Nellie: and other Stories.
The Elchester College Boys.
My First Cruise.
Lottie's White Frock.
Only Just Once.
The Little Peacemaker.
The Delft Jug. By Silverpen.

The "Baby's Album" Series. Four Books, each containing about 50 Illustrations. Price 6d. each; or cloth gilt, 1s. each.

Baby's Album.
Dolly's Album.

Fairy's Album
Pussy's Album.

Illustrated Books for the Little Ones. Containing interesting Stories. All Illustrated. 1s. each.

Indoors and Out.	Our Pretty Pets.
Some Farm Friends.	Our Schoolday Hours.
Those Golden Sands.	Creatures Tame.
Little Mothers & their Children.	Creatures Wild.

Shilling Story Books. All Illustrated, and containing Interesting Stories.

Thorns and Tangles.	Shag and Doll.
The Cuckoo in the Robin's Nest.	Aunt Lucia's Locket.
John's Mistake.	The Magic Mirror.
The History of Five Little Pitchers.	The Cost of Revenge.
	Clever Frank.
Diamonds in the Sand.	Among the Redskins.
Surly Bob.	The Ferryman of Brill.
The Giant's Cradle.	Harry Maxwell.
	A Banished Monarch.

"Little Folks" Painting Books. With Text, and Outline Illustrations for Water-Colour Painting. 1s. each.

Fruits and Blossoms for "Little Folks" to Paint.	Pictures to Paint.
	"Little Folks" Painting Book.
The "Little Folks" Proverb Painting Book.	"Little Folks" Nature Painting Book.
The "Little Folks" Illuminating Book.	Another "Little Folks" Painting Book.

Eighteenpenny Story Books. All Illustrated throughout.

Wee Little Rhymes.	Roses from Thorns.
Little One's Welcome.	Faith's Father.
Little Gossips.	By Land and Sea.
Ding Dong Bell.	The Young Berringtons.
Three Wee Ulster Lassies.	Jeff and Leff.
Little Queen Mab.	Tom Morris's Error.
Up the Ladder.	Worth more than Gold.
Dick's Hero; and other Stories.	"Through Flood—Through Fire;" and other Stories.
The Chip Boy.	
Raggles, Baggles, and the Emperor.	The Girl with the Golden Locks.
	Stories of the Olden Time.

The "Cosy Corner" Series. Story Books for Children. Each containing nearly ONE HUNDRED PICTURES. 1s. 6d. each.

See-Saw Stories.	Story Flowers for Rainy Hours.
Little Chimes for All Times.	Little Talks with Little People.
Wee Willie Winkie.	Chats for Small Chatterers.
Pet's Posy of Pictures and Stories.	Pictures for Happy Hours.
	Ups and Downs of a Donkey's
Dot's Story Book.	Life.

The "World in Pictures." Illustrated throughout. 2s. 6d. each.

A Ramble Round France.	The Eastern Wonderland (Japan).
All the Russias.	Glimpses of South America.
Chats about Germany.	Round Africa.
The Land of the Pyramids (Egypt).	The Land of Temples (India).
Peeps into China.	The Isles of the Pacific.

Two-Shilling Story Books. All Illustrated.

Clover Blossoms.	Maid Marjory.
Christmas Dreams.	The Four Cats of the Tippertons.
Stories of the Tower.	Marion's Two Homes.
Mr. Burke's Nieces.	Little Folks' Sunday Book.
May Cunningham's Trial.	Two Fourpenny Bits.
The Top of the Ladder: How to Reach it.	Poor Nelly.
Little Flotsam.	Tom Heriot.
Madge and her Friends.	Through Peril to Fortune.
The Children of the Court.	Aunt Tabitha's Waifs.
A Moonbeam Tangle.	In Mischief Again.

Half-Crown Story Books.

Arm-Chair Stories.
Little Hinges.
Margaret's Enemy.
Pen's Perplexities.
Notable Shipwrecks.
Golden Days.
Wonders of Common Things.
Little Empress Joan.
Truth will Out.

At the South Pole. *Cheap Edition.*
Soldier and Patriot (George Washington).
Picture of School Life and Boyhood.
The Young Man in the Battle of Life. By the Rev. Dr. Landels.
The True Glory of Woman. By the Rev. Dr. Landels.

Library of Wonders. Illustrated Gift-books for Boys. 2s. 6d. each.

Wonderful Adventures.
Wonders of Animal Instinct.
Wonders of Architecture.
Wonders of Acoustics.

Wonders of Water.
Wonderful Escapes.
Bodily Strength and Skill.
Wonderful Balloon Ascents.

Three and Sixpenny Library of Standard Tales, &c. All Illustrated and bound in cloth gilt. Crown 8vo. 3s. 6d. each.

Jane Austen and her Works.
Mission Life in Greece and Palestine.
The Dingy House at Kensington.
The Romance of Trade.
The Three Homes.
School Girls.
Deepdale Vicarage.

In Duty Bound.
The Half Sisters.
Peggy Oglivie's Inheritance.
The Family Honour.
Esther West.
Working to Win.
Krilof and his Fables. By W. R. S. Ralston, M.A.
Fairy Tales. By Prof. Morley.

The Home Chat Series. All Illustrated throughout. Fcap. 4to. Boards, 3s. 6d. each. Cloth, gilt edges, 5s. each.

Half-Hours with Early Explorers.
Stories about Animals.
Stories about Birds.

Paws and Claws.
Home Chat.
Peeps Abroad for Folks at Home.
Around and About Old England.

Books for the Little Ones.

Rhymes for the Young Folk. By William Allingham. Beautifully Illustrated. 3s. 6d.
The Little Doings of some Little Folks. By Chatty Cheerful. Illustrated 5s.
The Sunday Scrap Book. With One Thousand Scripture Pictures. Boards, 5s.; cloth, 7s. 6d.
Daisy Dimple's Scrap Book. Containing about 1,000 Pictures. Boards, 5s.; cloth gilt, 7s. 6d.
Little Folks' Picture Album. With 168 Large Pictures. 5s.
Little Folks' Picture Gallery. With 150 Illustrations. 5s.

The Old Fairy Tales. With Original Illustrations. Boards, 1s.; cloth, 1s. 6d.
My Diary. With 12 Coloured Plates and 366 Woodcuts. 1s.
The Story of Robin Hood. With Coloured Illustrations. 2s. 6d.
The Pilgrim's Progress. With Coloured Illustrations. 2s. 6d.
Wee Little Rhymes. 1s. 6d.
Little One's Welcome. 1s. 6d.
Little Gossips. 1s. 6d.
Ding Dong Bell. 1s. 6d.
Clover Blossoms. 2s.
Christmas Dreams. 2s.
Arm-Chair Stories. 2s. 6d.

Books for Boys.

Captain Trafalgar: A Story of the Mexican Gulf. By W. Westall. Illustrated. 5s.
Kidnapped. By R. L. Stevenson, 5s.
King Solomon's Mines. By H. Rider Haggard. 5s.
The Phantom City. By W. Westall 5s.
Treasure Island. By R. L. Stevenson. Illustrated. 5s.

Modern Explorers. By Thomas Frost. Illustrated. 5s.
Famous Sailors of Former Times. By Clements Markham. Illustrated. 2s. 6d.
Wild Adventures in Wild Places. By Dr. Gordon Stables, M.D., R.N. Illustrated. 5s.
Jungle, Peak, and Plain. By Dr. Gordon Stables, R.N. Illustrated. 5s.

CASSELL & COMPANY, Limited, London ; Paris, New York & Melbourne.